软式网球竞赛手册

荣礡　邵春　周末　著
中国网球协会　审定

人民体育出版社

图书在版编目（CIP）数据

软式网球竞赛手册 / 荣礴, 邵春, 周末著. -- 北京：人民体育出版社, 2022
　ISBN 978-7-5009-6183-3

　Ⅰ. ①软… Ⅱ. ①荣… ②邵… ③周… Ⅲ. ①网球运动—手册 Ⅳ. ①G845-62

中国版本图书馆CIP数据核字(2022)第110904号

*

人民体育出版社出版发行
北京中科印刷有限公司印刷
新 华 书 店 经 销

*

787×960　16开本　8.75印张　159千字
2022年12月第1版　2022年12月第1次印刷
印数：1—2,000册

*

ISBN 978-7-5009-6183-3
定价：49.00元

社址：北京市东城区体育馆路8号（天坛公园东门）
电话：67151482（发行部）　邮编：100061
传真：67151483　邮购：67118491
网址：www.psphpress.com

（购买本社图书，如遇有缺损页可与邮购部联系）

编 委 会

顾　　问：

白喜林　万建斌　谢弥青　吕　亮

编写组成员：

荣礴　中南林业科技大学

邵春　上海体育学院

周末　国家体育总局网球运动管理中心

前　言

软式网球运动，起源于传统网球运动，但其与传统网球运动又有许多不同之处。

软式网球自20世纪80年代传入我国以来，已有近40年的发展历史。随着该项目的普及，很多高校，特别是体育院校都开设了相关的课程，并成立了专业队伍。同时，软式网球作为亚运会正式比赛项目，也是我国竞技体育不可或缺的，且要力保夺牌展现我国实力的一个项目。

软式网球常规赛事日趋丰富，很多国际赛事在我国举办进一步推动了该项目的发展。

本书在中国网球协会指导下，参考国际软式网球联合会最新《软式网球竞赛规则》，以及亚洲软式网球联合会对赛事细则的相关规定，结合我国软式网球运动开展的具体情况编著而成。书中首先对软式网球运动的起源、发展及在我国的开展情况作了大致的介绍，而后对国际软式网球联合会制定的竞赛规则、裁判规则及赛事组织进行了详细的解读。根据该项目在国内开展的实际情况，书中增加了信任制比赛的执行规则，列举容易出错或与网球判罚不同且极易混淆的判例，并进行解答，以此加深读者印象，提升学习效果。书中最后附上国际软式网球联合会英文版规则供读者参考。该书的出版为提高我国软式网球运动水平，保障软式网球赛事在我国有序开展及裁判工作的正确执行，提供了规范与指导。

　　本书也适用于开设软式网球运动项目的高校进行教学及为软式网球赛事筹办提供参考，同时为需要考取软式网球裁判资格证书并从事软式网球裁判工作的人员或对软式网球运动感兴趣的读者提供学习用书。

　　本书编写如若存在不妥与疏漏，敬请广大读者及专家批评、指正，以便进一步修改、完善。

目 录

第一章　软式网球运动概述 （1）

第一节　软式网球运动 （1）

第二节　软式网球运动的起源与发展 （2）

第三节　中国软式网球运动的发展 （6）

第二章　竞赛规则 （12）

双打比赛 （12）

第一节　总则 （12）

1. 目的 （12）

第二节　软式网球场地 （13）

2. 软式网球场 （13）

3. 球场及球场界外空地 （13）

4. 球场及球场界外空地的表面 （13）

5. 球场 （13）

6. 界线名称及长度 （13）

7. 界线的颜色、宽度及长度 （14）

8. 球场界外空地 （14）

9. 网柱 （15）

10. 网柱的位置 （15）

11. 裁判员座椅 ……………………………………………（15）

第三节　设备 …………………………………………（15）

　　12. 球网 ……………………………………………………（15）

　　13. 球 ………………………………………………………（16）

　　14. 球拍 ……………………………………………………（17）

第四节　竞赛规则 ……………………………………（17）

　　15. 运动员行为准则 ………………………………………（17）

　　16. 比赛 ……………………………………………………（18）

　　17. 局数 ……………………………………………………（18）

　　18. 一局比赛的胜负 ………………………………………（18）

　　19. 一场比赛的胜负 ………………………………………（19）

　　20. 发球 ……………………………………………………（20）

　　21. 发球时机 ………………………………………………（20）

　　22. 发球方与接发球方 ……………………………………（20）

　　23. 发球位置 ………………………………………………（20）

　　24. 运动员发球 ……………………………………………（20）

　　25. 发球失误 ………………………………………………（21）

　　26. 重发球 …………………………………………………（21）

　　27. 发球失分 ………………………………………………（22）

　　28. 接发球 …………………………………………………（22）

　　29. 接发球的顺序 …………………………………………（23）

　　30. 接发球失分 ……………………………………………（23）

　　31. 发球/接发球和场区的选择 …………………………（23）

　　32. 发球/接发球和场区的交换 …………………………（23）

　　33. 发球/接发球顺序及场区交换错误 …………………（24）

　　34. 界内、界外球的判定 …………………………………（24）

35. 比赛进行中的失分 …………………………………（24）

36. 重赛球 ………………………………………………（26）

37. 暂停 …………………………………………………（26）

38. 禁止事项 ……………………………………………（26）

39. 弃权 …………………………………………………（27）

40. 禁止抗议的言行 ……………………………………（27）

41. 警告 …………………………………………………（28）

42. 取消比赛资格 ………………………………………（28）

43. 申诉 …………………………………………………（28）

44. 停止比赛与继续比赛 ………………………………（28）

45. 规则上的疑义 ………………………………………（29）

单打比赛 …………………………………………………（29）

1. 目的 …………………………………………………（29）

2. 球场 …………………………………………………（29）

3. 界线名称及长度 ……………………………………（30）

4. 发球与接球 …………………………………………（30）

5. 比赛局数 ……………………………………………（30）

第三章　裁判规则 ………………………………………（31）

第一节　总则 ……………………………………………（31）

1. 目的 …………………………………………………（31）

第二节　裁判团 …………………………………………（31）

2. 裁判团 ………………………………………………（31）

3. 裁判长 ………………………………………………（32）

4. 场地监督 ……………………………………………（32）

3

5. 裁判员 …………………………………………………（32）

6. 裁判员的任务 …………………………………………（32）

第三节　裁判员的职责 ……………………………………（33）

7. 裁判员须知 ……………………………………………（33）

8. 裁判员的责任区域 ……………………………………（33）

9. 裁判员位置 ……………………………………………（34）

10. 宣告 …………………………………………………（36）

11. 手势 …………………………………………………（36）

12. 球点的确认 …………………………………………（39）

13. 判定的协调 …………………………………………（39）

14. 最终判定 ……………………………………………（40）

15. 改判 …………………………………………………（40）

16. 中止比赛 ……………………………………………（40）

17. 计分错误 ……………………………………………（40）

18. 弃权 …………………………………………………（40）

19. 口头警告 ……………………………………………（41）

20. 正式警告 ……………………………………………（41）

21. 取消比赛资格 ………………………………………（41）

22. 禁止更换裁判员 ……………………………………（42）

第四节　比赛进程 …………………………………………（42）

23. 裁判工作程序 ………………………………………（42）

24. 计分表 ………………………………………………（46）

第四章　竞赛组织 ……………………………………………（48）

第一节　总则 ………………………………………………（48）

1. 目的 ……………………………………………………（48）

2. 竞赛规程 ……………………………………………………（48）

第二节　比赛场地设施 ……………………………………………（49）

　　3. 场地设施 …………………………………………………（49）

第三节　竞赛事宜 …………………………………………………（50）

　　4. 竞赛项目 …………………………………………………（50）

　　5. 竞赛日程 …………………………………………………（50）

　　6. 报名资格 …………………………………………………（50）

　　7. 报名方法 …………………………………………………（50）

　　8. 适用于本规则的特殊情况 ………………………………（50）

　　9. 竞赛制度 …………………………………………………（51）

　　10. 循环赛中名次的判定 ……………………………………（51）

　　11. 循环赛中弃权的处理办法 ………………………………（52）

　　12. 弃权 ………………………………………………………（52）

　　13. 取消资格 …………………………………………………（52）

　　14. 赛程编排 …………………………………………………（53）

　　15. 比赛成绩的记录 …………………………………………（55）

　　16. 参赛资格 …………………………………………………（55）

　　17. 比赛用球 …………………………………………………（55）

　　18. 兴奋剂检测 ………………………………………………（56）

　　19. 医疗监护 …………………………………………………（56）

　　20. 奖励办法 …………………………………………………（56）

　　21. 参赛经费 …………………………………………………（56）

　　22. 领队会议 …………………………………………………（56）

　　23. 竞赛官员 …………………………………………………（56）

　　24. 裁判团 ……………………………………………………（56）

　　25. 安全保障 …………………………………………………（57）

26. 入场费 ……………………………………………………（57）

27. 赞助商 ……………………………………………………（57）

第五章　软式网球信任制比赛裁判方法 ………………（61）

1. 信任制比赛巡场裁判员工作程序 ………………………（61）

2. 信任制比赛运动员须知 …………………………………（62）

3. 信任制比赛巡场裁判员操作步骤 ………………………（63）

第六章　判例分析 …………………………………………（64）

1. 判例 ………………………………………………………（64）

2. 解答 ………………………………………………………（72）

附录 ……………………………………………………………（75）

附录1　软式网球比赛术语 …………………………………（76）

附录2　软式网球比赛记分表 ………………………………（80）

附录3　竞赛器材清单 ………………………………………（81）

附录4　裁判长、副裁判长及仲裁具体工作任务 …………（82）

附录5　国际软式网球联合会规则（英文版）……………（84）

参考文献 ………………………………………………………（125）

第一章　软式网球运动概述

第一节　软式网球运动

软式网球运动起源于日本，它是在传统网球运动基础上发展起来的一个新兴运动项目。

软式网球与传统网球有一些共性，但也有一些区别，最主要的区别是软式网球使用的是更加柔软的橡胶球，"软式网球"因此而得名。

除此以外，这项运动也随之发展出一些独特之处。例如，一支更轻、更灵活的球拍、较低的拍线磅数、独特的击球技术及利用球的柔软性而衍生出对球的控制方法，这些都充分利用了球的柔软性。你可以用最舒适的感觉来用力击球，并且发现对球的控制也很容易。

在比赛中，你可以看到运动员令人惊叹的击球技术及令人印象深刻的战术运用。运动员击球的速度、敏捷的身手和完美的击球时机都让人兴奋。双打项目中运动员之间的默契配合，使得这项运动更加受欢迎。

因为使用了更为柔软的球、轻巧的球拍、较低的拍线磅数，以及在球场上弹跳后球的速度减缓，从而使每个人不论性别和年龄，都能享受到软式网球的乐趣。上至退休的老人，下至几岁的孩童，每个人都能参与到软式网球运动中。"人人都可以打软式网球"（Soft Tennis for Anyone and Everyone）精准地概括了这一点（图1-1）。

图1-1　正在进行的女子双打比赛

第二节　软式网球运动的起源与发展

软式网球诞生于日本明治维新初期，当时西方的传教士、商人将草地网球带进了日本，于是在日本繁华的城市中便开始有了网球运动。

但因为当时日本还不具备制作网球和球拍的条件，进口又比较昂贵，学校开展网球运动受到了限制。经过实践，他们发现游戏用的橡胶球可以代替网球，于是三田橡胶公司开始制作软式网球专用的橡胶球，并在全国推广，由此便在日本诞生了软式网球。1898年，软式网球在日本被列为国内正式比赛项目。1904年，由东京高师、高商、庆应、早稻田四所大学发起制定了统一的比赛规则。1923年，举办了第一届全日本软式网球锦标赛。随后，日本把软式网球介绍到韩国和中国台湾省。

1955年，日本成立"亚洲软式网球联盟"。1956年，该联盟举办亚洲软式网球锦标赛，至1973年共举办9届（图1-2）。为了在世界范围内进一步推广软式网球，1973年，亚洲软式网球联盟解散，组成了世界软式网球联盟（ISTF），决定自1975年开始每两年举办一次世界软式网球锦标赛（取代了亚洲锦标赛），首届比赛在美国夏威夷举行。1988年，重建亚洲软式网球联合会（ASTF），并恢复亚洲软式网球锦标赛，每四年举办一届（参与成员见表1-1）。1990年，在北京举办的第11届亚运会上，软式网球运动被列为表演项目。1994年，在日本广岛举行的第12届亚运会上，软式网球运动被列为正式比赛项目。1991年后，为了配合亚运会及亚锦赛的开展，世锦赛也改为每四年举办一次。

图1-2　20世纪60年代的软式网球赛事

表1-1　亚洲软式网球联合会（ASTF）成员

序号	成员/英文缩写		组织名称
1	孟加拉国（Bangladesh）	BAN	孟加拉软式网球协会（Bangladesh Soft Tennis Association）
2	柬埔寨（Cambodia）	CAM	柬埔寨软式网球协会（Cambodia Soft Tennis Association）
3	中国（China）	CHN	中国网球协会（Chinese Tennis Association）
4	韩国（Korea）	KOR	韩国软式网球协会（Korea Soft Tennis Association）
5	中国香港（Hong Kong，China）	HKG	香港业余软式网球协会（Hong Kong Amateur Soft Tennis Association）
6	印度（India）	IND	印度业余软式网球联合会（Amateur Soft Tennis Federation of Indea）
7	印度尼西亚（Indonesia）	INA	印度尼西亚软式网球协会（Indonesian Soft Tennis Association）
8	日本（Japan）	JPN	日本软式网球协会（Japan Soft Tennis Association）

（续表）

序号	成员/英文缩写		组织名称
9	哈萨克斯坦（Kazakhstan）	KZK	哈萨克斯坦共和国软式网球联合会（Soft Tennis Federation of The Republic of Kazakhstan）
10	吉尔吉斯斯坦（Kyrgyzstan）	KGZ	吉尔吉斯斯坦共和国软网球联合会（Soft Tennis Federation of The Republic of Kyrgyzstan）
11	老挝（Laos）	LAO	老挝软式网球协会（Laos Soft Tennis Association）
12	马来西亚（Malaysia）	MAS	马来西亚软式网球协会（Malaysia Soft Tennis Association）
13	马尔代夫（Maldives）	MDV	马尔代夫软式网球协会（Soft Tennis Association of Maldives）
14	蒙古国（Mongolia）	MGL	蒙古软式网球协会（Mongolian Soft Tennis Association）
15	尼泊尔（Nepal）	NEP	尼泊尔软式网球协会（Nepal Soft Tennis Association）
16	巴基斯坦（Pakistan）	PAK	巴基斯坦软式网球协会（Pakistan Soft Tennis Association）
17	菲律宾（Philippines）	PHI	菲律宾软式网球协会（Philippine Soft Tennis Association）
18	朝鲜（D.P.R Korea）	PRK	朝鲜民主主义人民共和国网球协会（Tennis Association The Democratic People's Republic of Korea）
19	中国澳门（Macao, China）	MAC	澳门软式网球协会（Macau Soft Tennis Association）
20	中国台北（Chinese Taipei）	TPE	中国台北软式网球协会（Chinese Taipei Soft Tennis Association）
21	泰国（Thailand）	THA	泰国软式网球协会（Thailand Soft Tennis Association）
22	塔吉克斯坦（Tajikistan）	TJK	塔吉克斯坦软式网球联合会（Tajikistan Soft Tennis Federation）
23	越南（Vietnam）	VIE	越南软式网球联合会（Vietnam Soft Tennis Federation）

随着软式网球运动的发展及推广，目前该项目已在世界许多国家和地区开展起来，特别是在日本、韩国，以及中国的台湾省，软式网球非常普及，群众基础广泛。在这些地区，软式网球是一项职业化的运动，有职业俱乐部和职业联赛的支持。近年来，软式网球在蒙古国、菲律宾、印度、尼泊尔等国家发展也很迅猛，在各项赛事中实力已不容小觑。此外，欧美也有很多国家参与到此项运动中来（图1-3、图1-4）。

图1-3　2019年举办的第23届国际软式网球联合会大会

图1-4　第16届世界软式网球锦标赛开幕式

除了上述的亚运会、世界锦标赛、亚洲锦标赛以外，软式网球其他赛事也如火如荼地开展起来。例如，定期举行的亚洲杯、亚洲青少年锦标赛（图1-5）、世界青少年锦标赛、欧洲软式网球锦标赛、东南亚软式网球锦标赛，以及中日韩运动会等，还有广岛杯、中国杯、韩国杯、波兰杯、印尼杯等各国举办的国际赛事。赛事的开展，促进了各国官员、运动员、裁判员之间的交流，使该项目得到进一步的推广、普及和提高。

图1-5　第1届亚洲青少年软式网球锦标赛

第三节　中国软式网球运动的发展

1986年4月，软式网球运动进入中国。当时，日本东京女子体育大学与沈阳体育学院建立校际关系，软式网球作为日本东京女子体育大学与沈阳体院之间的交流项目而引进中国。1986年下半年，在国家体委有关部门的重视与扶植下，软式网球运动在全国部分体育院校中迅速得到开展。从此，软式网球运动不仅在我国扎下了根，而且在各方面的努力下逐步地发展成长。

1987年4月，我国成立了中国软式网球协会，时任国家体委副主任张彩珍任该协会的主席（为进一步深化社团和协会的改革，切实加强协会建设，提升协会管理能力，在改革中找到新的发展动力，2018年，注销原中国软式网球协会，其所有工作并入中国网球协会统一管理）。在中国软式网球协会的倡导与推动下，软式网球运动得到了普及，运动技术水平也得到了极大的提高。1987年8月20—25日，我国在昆明海埂训练基地举办了首届全国软式网球邀请赛和中日大学生对抗赛。参加本届比赛的有北京体育学院、西安体育学院、武汉体育学院、成都体育学院、天津体育学院、北京体育师范学院、沈阳体育学院等单位的121名男、女运动员。赛会进行了男、女团体和男、女单项（双打）比赛，并选拔出优秀运动员联合组成中国大学生代表队与日本大学生代表队进行了对抗赛。通过这次比赛，交流了技艺，锻炼了队伍，培养了裁判，为我国软式网球运动的进一步发展奠定了基础。

1988年，我国将这项赛事正式命名为全国软式网球锦标赛。原中国软式网球协会决定，每年举行一次全国锦标赛，截至2019年共举办了33届。为了增加各队运动员间的球技交流机会，迅速提高运动技术水平，从1995年开始，我国又增设了全国软式网球青少年锦标赛和全国软式网球冠军赛，截至2019年两项赛事均已举办了25届，还有中国杯这项国际赛事也已举办了18届，这些举措为我国软式网球运动的进一步发展和软网运动水平的提高提供了良好的条件。

随着国际、国内赛事的增多，对专业裁判人员的需求也越来越大。为配合2013年东亚运动会软式网球项目的举行，国家体育总局网球运动管理中心于2012年在山东体育学院举办了第一届软式网球国家级裁判员培训班，截至2019年共进行了3批次的软式网球国家级裁判员培训及考核工作，培养出国家级裁判员63人，其中有23人通过考核荣升为软式网球国际级裁判。在中国网球协会的组织下，大家齐心协力，为保障各项软网赛事在中国的顺利开展，贡献了自己的一份力量（图1-6、图1-7）。

图1-6　国际软式网球联合会前主席朴相何先生给卿尚霖先生颁发国际软式网球联合会副主席证书

图1-7 第16届世界软式网球锦标赛技术官员合影

中国网球协会为加大软式网球运动的发展力度，还采取了"请进来、走出去"的方法，不仅与各国运动员进行广泛交流，还经常派出教练员赴日受训，并聘请日本专家来我国讲学、任教。这些活动使得我国教练员水平不断提高，运动技术水平不断提升，在第16届世界软式网球锦标赛上，我国取得男子单打银牌，女子单打斩获冠、季军及混合双打第三名，女子团体第三名的可喜成绩，充分显示了我国软式网球运动的普及和技术水平的提高，充分证明了我国的软式网球运动水平已立于世界强国之林，实力不容小觑（图1-8～图1-11，表1-2）。

图1-8 2016年中国杯国际软式网球锦标赛中国队领队、教练员、运动员合影

图1-9　第16届世界软式网球锦标赛中国队教练员、运动员合影

图1-10　我国选手辛雅妮（左）、赵蕾（右）获得2010年广州亚运会双打第三名

图1-11　第16届世界软式网球锦标赛女子单打颁奖仪式

表1-2　中国软式网球队近年世界大赛成绩

序号	赛事名称	时间（年/月）	举办地	项目	成绩
1	第16届世界软式网球锦标赛	2019.10	中国·台州	男子单打 女子单打 混合双打 女子团体	第二名 牛巨达 第一名 谢思琪 第三名 于元祎 第三名 谭浩 谢思琪 第三名 谢思琪 于元祎 马玥 付晓晨 江睿婕 李沁芳
2	第3届世界青少年软式网球锦标赛	2018.11	韩国·顺天	男子单打U-18 女子单打U-21 男子双打U-18 女子团体	第二名 牛巨达 第三名 马玥 第三名 宋泽昱 牛巨达 第三名 王宇菲 马玥 李思慧 胡颖 李沁芳
3	第18届亚运会	2018.8	印度尼西亚·雅加达-巨港	女子单打 女子团体	第三名 于元祎 第三名 于元祎 王宇菲 冯子轩 马玥 刘银
4	第8届亚洲软式网球锦标赛	2016.11	日本·千叶	女子单打 混合双打	第二名 冯子轩 第三名 周末 王宇菲
5	第15届世界软式网球锦标赛	2015.11	印度·德里	男子单打 女子单打 女子团体	第二名 周末 第二名 陈慧 第三名 陈慧 钟怡 冯子轩 陈禹希 张伊婵 王韵茹
6	第17届亚运会	2014.9	韩国·仁川	男子单打 女子单打 混合双打 男子团体 女子团体	第三名 周末 第二名 陈慧 第二名 周末 陈慧 第三名 周末 施小霖 林成伟 张羽圣 李泽 第三名 陈慧 辛雅妮 钟怡 冯子轩 刘格

（续表）

序号	赛事名称	时间（年/月）	举办地	项目	成绩
7	第6届东亚运动会	2013.10	中国·天津	男子单打 女子单打 混合双打 男子团体 女子团体	第三名 焦旸 第二名 赵蕾 第三名 史博 赵蕾 第三名 史博 焦旸 潘一夫 李一龙 周末 第三名 赵蕾 陈慧 辛雅妮 周纽萱 冯子轩
8	第14届世界软式网球锦标赛	2011.10	韩国·闻庆	混合双打 混合双打 女子团体	第二名 史博 赵蕾 第三名 焦旸 辛雅妮 第三名 赵蕾 刘格 辛雅妮 周纽萱 陈慧 胡锐
9	第16届亚运会	2010.11	中国·广州	女子单打 女子双打 男子团体 女子团体	第一名 赵蕾 第三名 辛雅妮 赵蕾 第三名 焦旸 陈明栋 史博 李翔 柴进 第三名 赵蕾 高彤 郝洁 邱思思 辛雅妮

第二章　竞赛规则

双打比赛

第一节　总则

1. 目的

为保障软式网球比赛（双打比赛）的进行，特制定所必须遵守的事项。

图2-1　软式网球双打比赛

第二节 软式网球场地

2. 软式网球场

软式网球场由球场、球场界外空地，以及网柱、球网、裁判台等组成。

3. 球场及球场界外空地

球场及球场界外空地为平坦的同一地面，并保持表面的清洁，以免对比赛进行造成影响。室外场地在不影响比赛的前提下，允许有轻微的倾斜用于排水。

4. 球场及球场界外空地的表面

球场及球场界外空地的表面、室外球场应以黏土、人工草皮或全天候型的化学材质为主，室内球场则以木板、人工草皮、硬质橡胶、化学材质等为表面。

5. 球场

软式网球场地为长方形，长23.77米，双打比赛的场地宽度为10.97米。

场地由一条球网从中间处分隔开，球网悬挂在网绳或金属绳上，附着在1.07米高的两根网柱上。球网应充分伸展开，填满两个网柱之间的空间，网孔的大小应确保球不能从中间穿过。

从球场地面上1米的高度测量，每片场地照明度不低于500勒[克斯]。灯光的光线应均匀地照在场地上，光线柔和不刺眼。灯杆的位置，应选择安装在不影响打球的地方。室内球场的顶高从球网处地面量起，高度至少为9.14米，如从挡球板地面处量起，高度应不低于4.87米。

6. 界线名称及长度

球场的区域、界线名称及长度如图2-2所示，球场两端的界线称为底线，两侧的界线称为边线。

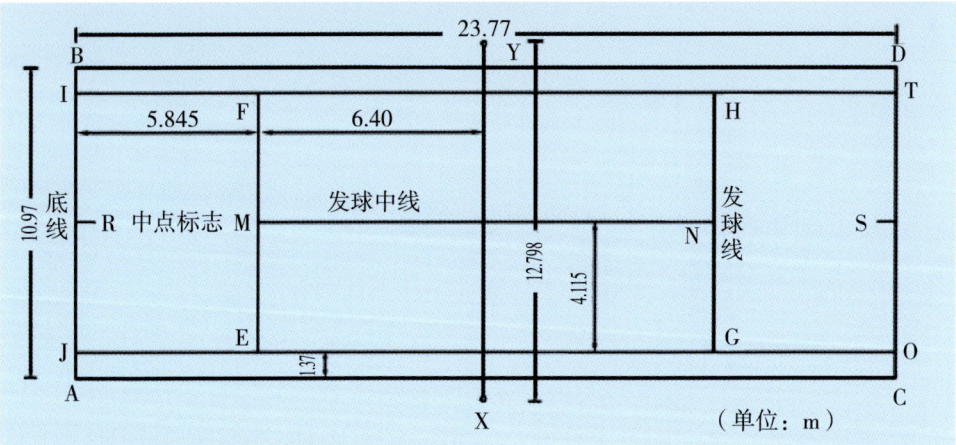

界线名称	符号	长度
边线	A-C/B-D（双打）、I-J/T-O（单打）	23.77米
底线	A-B/C-D（双打）、I-J/T-O（单打）	10.97、8.23米
发球边线	E-G/F-H	12.80米
发球底线	E-F/G-H	8.23米
发球中线	M-N	12.80米
中点标志	R、S	0.15米

图2-2 软式网球场地平面图

注：中点标志R、S是从底线内沿向球场内测量，长度为0.15米。

7. 界线的颜色、宽度及长度

场地上所有的线应为白色，宽度为5厘米以上6厘米以内。底线的宽度为大于5厘米，小于10厘米。

8. 球场界外空地

（1）软式网球场地原则上底线后方应有8米以上，边线外侧应有6米以上的空间（图2-3）。

（2）如有两片以上的球场并排时，原则上紧邻的两片球场的边线与边线之间距离应在5米以上。

图2-3　软式网球比赛场地

9. 网柱

网柱的边长/直径应大于7.5厘米，不超过15厘米。

注：网柱外侧附属的紧网器应视为网柱的一部分。

10. 网柱的位置

（1）网柱应垂直固定在球场边线中央的外侧，且离相应边线的距离相等的位置上。

（2）两网柱外侧之间的距离为12.80米，网柱的高度为1.07米。如条件达不到要求的情况下，可小于1.07米，但不能小于1.06米。

11. 裁判员座椅

裁判员座椅的高度原则上为1.50米，放置在球场边线外靠近网柱处，与网柱的水平距离为0.6米。

第三节　设备

12. 球网

球网规格如下。

（1）颜色：黑色。

（2）高度：1.07米，在条件达不到要求的情况下，高度可小于1.07米，但不能小于1.06米（球网拉成水平后，从边线上测量的高度应为1.06～1.07米）。

（3）长度：12.65米。

（4）网孔：边长不超过3.5厘米的方形。

（5）钢丝绳：长度为15米，标准直径为4.5毫米。

（6）球网上方两面均应被宽度为5～6厘米的网边白布包缝。

（7）球网两端紧接于网柱，下端必须与球场地面接触。

13. 球

球应是充有空气的橡胶制品，一般以白色为主，其规格如下：

（1）球的弹性：在比赛场地上从1.5米高度自然落下，反弹后至最高点时，其底部的高度在70～80厘米。

（2）重量：球的重量为30～31克。

（3）直径：球的直径为6.6±0.1（厘米）。

注：比赛用球有白色、黄色两种，如大会竞赛规程对用球颜色并未有特殊规定，原则上使用白色（图2-4）。球因使用后自然变色时，应视为与使用前颜色相同。

图2-4　软式网球

14. 球拍

（1）球拍在设计上，两面应有相同特性，拍框须安装拍线，击球面必须为平面，拍线安装后大体上均匀一致（图2-5）。

图2-5　软式网球球拍

（2）球拍可以是任何材料，任何重量，尺寸、形状不限。
（3）拍线安装在球拍上必须相互交叉。
（4）不得使用能使球产生过度变化的拍线。

注：当拍面附加其他特殊装置，可能使球在击打时产生特别的变化而影响对方击球时，该球拍能否使用由裁判长负责判定。

第四节　竞赛规则

15. 运动员行为准则

运动员应相互尊重，并遵守下列行为准则：
（1）运动员不得有大声喧哗、吼叫或使对手感到不愉快的言行。
（2）运动员自始至终不得无故中断比赛（当上一分或上一局结束，下一分或下一局开始前，交换场地或决胜局开始前，15分制比赛10分球结束后交换场地时，间隔时间均不能超过1分钟）并禁止以下行为：

　　a. 对方已做好接球准备而故意不发球，或对方准备发球而故意不做接球准备；

　　b. 故意拖延比赛的行为；

　　c. 在双打比赛中，分与分或局间与同伴长时间相互交流或休息而影响比赛进行；

　　d. 每局结束后，在允许时间内没有及时准备进行下一局比赛；

　　e. 在决胜局中交换场区时有休息行为；

　　f. 修补球拍而中断比赛的行为。

　　（3）运动员应遵循裁判员的指示进行比赛。

　　注：比赛中运动员喧哗、吼叫、中断比赛等，其程度是否对比赛造成影响由该场裁判员判定。

16. 比赛

　　（1）运动员在比赛中始终遵守竞赛规则，光明磊落、公平公正、有始有终地进行比赛。

　　（2）双打比赛应由两名运动员搭配为一队，每名运动员各自使用一支球拍参加比赛。

　　（3）两对运动员应分别站于球网两侧轮流交替击球来进行比赛。

17. 局数

　　（1）比赛原则上采用七局制或九局制。

　　（2）比赛也可采用更少的局数或分数来决定胜负，如15分制、三局制、五局制或采用多盘制比赛，将15分制、三局制、五局制、七局制或九局制赛计为一盘，一共举行三盘或五盘的比赛。

18. 一局比赛的胜负

　　（1）先赢4分者胜一局。但双方各得3分时为平分（Deuce），比赛遵循以下原则进行：

a. 平分之后赢1分者为"领先"，连续赢2分者为胜一局；

b. 如果领先者未能连续赢得下一分时，为再平分（Deuce again），处理方式与平分相同；

（2）在七局制比赛中，双方各赢三局时，第七局为决胜局（Final game），应按下列方式处理：

a. 决胜局中先赢7分者赢得决胜局且赢得该场比赛；

b. 当双方各赢6分时，为平分（Deuce），比赛则适用于第18条第（1）款的规定。

在三局制双方各赢一局时，五局制双方各赢二局及九局制双方各赢四局时，也以同样方式处理。

（3）在15分制比赛中，以先赢15分者为胜，但双方各赢14分时为平分（Deuce），比赛则适用于第18条第（1）款的规定。

19. 一场比赛的胜负

（1）3局以上奇数局的比赛，先赢得过半数局数者获胜。

（2）3盘以上奇数盘的比赛，每局以先赢得过半数局数者获胜，先赢得过半数盘数者，为该场比赛获胜者（图2-6）。

图2-6　软式网球记分牌

20. 发球

（1）发球是从发球运动员用一只手将球抛出（为了发球而将球抛离手掌）的瞬间开始至该球落到球场（包括场外）之前，以球拍击出球的瞬间为止。如果挥拍未击中球，则视为已完成发球动作，其球拍与球可能接触的时间点由主裁判认定。

（2）只能使用一只手的运动员，发球时可用球拍将球抛起发球。

21. 发球时机

发球应该在主裁判做出相应的呼报，并确认接球方已做好接发球准备后进行。

注：进行发球时，必须具备以下两项前提条件：

（1）主裁判的呼报（分数的呼报、重发球或失误等的呼报）后；

（2）确认接球方已做好接球准备。

如果未具备这两项前提条件，即使只缺一项，该发球即为重发球（Let），因此主裁判必须马上呼报该球为重发球，无论其有效或失误。

22. 发球方与接发球方

双方运动员面对球网各站一个场区，发球一方称为发球方，接球一方称为接发球方。

23. 发球位置

发球员应站在底线后、边线及中点标志线的假定延长线之间进行发球。

24. 运动员发球

（1）发球运动员发球，从中点标志线的右侧区域开始，将球发到对方对角发球区内，下一分发球换到左边开始，以此顺序进行。

（2）在同一局中，两名运动员应轮流各发2分球，并在该局中不得变更发球顺序。

25. 发球失误

（1）如有下列情况，均为发球失误：

a. 发球未能落到有效的发球区内，但竞赛规则第26条的重发球情况除外；

b. 发球员已有发球动作，将球抛至空中后而未击球；

c. 发球方发球时将两只球同时离手，或球离手后球拍尚未击到该球而另一只球掉落；

注：放在口袋中的球掉落时不受此限制。

d. 发球时，球拍与球有两次以上接触；

注：下手切削发球时不适用于该规定，球拍与球虽有较长时间的摩擦，但仍应视为一次接触。

e. 所发的球碰到球网或网柱后，球尚未落到对方球场、球场界外空地或碰到裁判椅、挡网等之前，有下列情况者：

　i. 接触到本方运动员的球拍（包括脱手的球拍）、身体或衣物（包括发球员所有的穿戴物如帽子、毛巾、眼镜等，以下类同）；

　ii. 发球运动员的球拍（包括脱手的球拍）、身体或衣物触网或过网（包括网柱）。

f. 发球运动员发球时（从抛球开始）触到底线、边线或中点标志（及其假定延长线外的地面）或进入球场内时属于脚误（Foot fault），但发球运动员在空间越过则不属于脚误。

注：所发的球直接触碰到下列任何一项时，均为发球失误：

i. 裁判员；

ii. 裁判员座椅或其他附属的设施或设备；

iii. 搭档的球拍、身体或衣物。

（2）发球方如果第一次发球失误，应进行第二次发球。

26. 重发球

（1）如有以下情况应判重发球：

a. 发球员违反竞赛规则第21条规定时，但必须由主裁判认定；

注：不论所发的球是否有效，均应重发球。

b.所发的球触网或触网柱后出现以下情况：

i.球落到对方有效的发球区内；

ii.球尚未落到球场、球场界外空地或碰到裁判椅、挡网等之前，触到接发球方的球拍（包括脱手的球拍）、身体或衣物；

iii.接发球方的球拍（包括脱手的球拍）、身体或衣物触网或过网。

c.接发球运动员未完成接球之前，有下列情况发生时，由主裁判认定（注："未完成接球前"指发球者将球抛离手掌的瞬间到接球者将有效发球在第二次落地前，击回给对方这段时间）：

i.由于裁判员判罚错误而影响击球时（注：此款仅适用于接球者实际上能还击对方发球，但由于裁判员的判定而影响比赛的情况。如果是对方发球为快速犀利的有效球，不论裁判员是否做出错误的判定，主裁判认定接球者根本无法还击的状况，则不在此限制内——此时若裁判员出现误判，该球不可判为重发球，而应改判为有效球，接球方失分。能否还击或误判是否影响比赛的进行，则由主裁判认定）；

ii.由于突发事件而影响比赛或其他球场的球，以及受到与比赛无关第三者等的妨碍而中断接球（注：是指该球场的使用球移动到他处，被比赛无关第三者掷回时，仅限于当时，视为非该球场的使用球）；

iii.双方同时发生失分时（注：例如，接球方在有效发球第二次落地无法还击的同时，发球方中的一人触网）。

d.主裁判认为必须重发球的其他情况。

（2）当发球成为重发球时，该球必须重发。

27.发球失分

第一次发球与第二次发球连续失误时称为双误（Double faults），应判为失1分。

28.接发球

接发球是指将有效发球在第一次反弹后尚未第二次落地前，用球拍将球击回去。

29. 接发球的顺序

接发球的顺序如下：

（1）接发球运动员各自在右或左发球区接球，同一局中不得更换接球次序。

（2）接发球必须从右区开始，再换到左区的顺序依次交替轮流接发球。

30. 接发球失分

接发球时有下列情况者应失1分：

（1）未能将有效发球回击到对方场地内。

（2）发球未落地之前，球直接触到接发球方任意一人的球拍、身体或衣物的直接球（Direct）。

（3）有效发球在第二次落地前触及到接球运动员同伴的球拍、身体或衣物的干扰（Interfere）。

（4）发球后接发球运动员尚未完成接球之前，其同伴进入该发球区的干扰（Interfere）。

（5）违反竞赛规则第29条第（1）款时应判干扰（Interfere），但只限于该分。

31. 发球/接发球和场区的选择

运动员在比赛开始前，要做好发球/接发球和场区的选择。

32. 发球/接发球和场区的交换

（1）发球方和接发球方，除决胜局外，每一局结束后与对方相互交换发球。奇数局结束后进行场区的交换。

（2）在决胜局中，每2分球后与对方交换发球，最初2分球结束后及以后每4分球结束后交换场地。发球及接发球在决胜局中按以下方式进行：

a. 双方每名运动员须轮流连续发2分球；

b. 按原来的发球顺序，轮到发球的发球方中任何一人发第1、第2分球；

c. 第3、第4分球的发球，由原先接球方中接第1分球的运动员发球，而原先发球方中发第1、第2分球的运动员接第3分球；

d. 第5、第6分球的发球，由决胜局中发最初2分球运动员的同伴发球；

e. 第7、第8分球的发球，由接发球方发第3、第4分球运动员的同伴发球；

f. 以后的发球及接发球的顺序按以上条款b至e已定的顺序进行；

g. 在该局比赛中发球及接发球顺序不得更改。

33. 发球/接发球顺序及场区交换错误

（1）发现发球/接发球及场区交换错误时，如果是在这一分开始前，应立即更正；如果是在比赛中（活球期）才发现错误，应在下一分开始前更正，先前所得的分数均有效；在比赛中即使发现错误也不得中断比赛。

a. 发球方交换错误（Change service）或场区交换错误（Change sides）时；

b. 与同伴发球次序错误（Rotation change）时；

c. 发球区的顺序选择错误（Rotation change）时。

（2）第一次发球失误后，发现错误应及时更正，更正后从第一发球开始。

注：在比赛中，即使发现错误，运动员也不得中断比赛，如违反，则中断比赛的一方失分；发球时接发球方发现错误，可即刻请求暂停而不接球，中断比赛是被允许的，如果是在接发球后，则中断比赛的一方失分。

34. 界内、界外球的判定

（1）不论界内球或界外球，都必须以球的落点来判断。

（2）凡落点触碰到场地界线上的球都为界内球。

35. 比赛进行中的失分

比赛中有下列情况者，应判失1分。重发球或第一次发球失误不在此限定内。

（1）击球未直接过网（不呼报）。球从网孔、网与网柱之间或从球网下方穿过时判为穿越球（Through），但下列情况不在此限定内：

a. 所击的球碰到球网或网柱，但进入对方有效场区时；

b. 所击的球绕过网柱外侧或触到网柱外侧而落入对方有效场区时。

（2）击出的球落在界外，或直接触到该场裁判员、裁判员座椅或其他附属设施时判界外球（Out）。

（3）球在第二次落地前，无法用球拍有效还击到对方场区时判为两跳（Two bounces），包括球在第二次落地前，触及了该场地的裁判员、裁判员座椅或其他附属设施。但是当对方回球落入球场又反向弹回触到球网或网柱，在第二次落地前将其回击到对方场区内时，应判为有效还击。

（4）球触及运动员身体或衣物时判为触身球（Body touch）。

（5）运动员的球拍、身体或衣物如有以下情形时：

a. 运动员挥拍未击中球，并造成球拍越过球网（包括球网的假定延长线）或网柱判为过网（Net over）；

b. 触及球网、网柱或因风吹、球的击打使球网鼓起而触及运动员判为触网（Net touch）；

c. 触及该球场裁判员或裁判员座椅时判为触及（Touch）；

d. 触到对方场区或对方运动员的球拍、身体或衣物时判为干扰（Interfere）；但由于击球后的惯性，球拍随球过网或触到对方界外空地未构成干扰时，则不属于干扰。

（6）击球时球拍与球有两次以上的接触判为连击（Dribble），或球在球拍上有停滞现象时应判为持球（Carry）。

注：切球的击球方法，其球拍与球的接触应视为一次。

（7）由于击球时球触及拍框而未能有效回球应判为擦拍球（Tip）。

（8）击球前球拍离手，抛拍击球判为干扰（Interfere）。

（9）比赛进行中球击到球场内的另一球（仅限于该场地使用的球，如果比赛中该球在所在的场区，由于风吹而移动到不同场区的情况也包括在内，但如果主裁判认为运动员是故意将该球移动到对方场区内时，则可视为干扰。）及触到运动员掉落的帽子、毛巾等，而无法有效回击时（不呼报）。

（10）运动员的球拍、帽子、毛巾或其他物品离开运动员而直接触及球网或网柱时应判为触网（Net touch），包括球拍落地后再触及球网或网柱。

（11）运动员为了将掉落在球场内或界外空地上的帽子或毛巾（球不在此限制），以手、球拍或脚将其抛远，从而造成这些物品接触到该场地的裁判员、裁判员座椅判为触及（Touch），触及球网、网柱判为触网（Net touch）。

（12）运动员的球拍、帽子、毛巾等触及对手的球拍或衣物或进入对方场区判为干扰（Interfere）。

（13）造成明显妨碍对方击球的情况应判为干扰（Interfere），如果球被夹在球拍拍颈的三角形区域时，则判为持球（Carry），判其失分。

注：条例中的裁判员座椅及裁判员是指该场比赛的裁判员座椅及裁判员。

36. 重赛球

在比赛进行中如有下列情况时，则应视为重赛球（No count），比赛应重新从第一发球开始（注：重发球除外）：

（1）因裁判员的误判而影响比赛进行时（注：是指运动员实际上可以回球的情况下，因裁判员的误判而使比赛中断，不论裁判员已做任何判定，该球很明显为制胜分时，主裁判须更正其判罚，能否判直接得分由主裁判认定）。

（2）因意外事故发生而导致比赛中断时，或其他场地的球（包括该场地使用的比赛球），被比赛无关的第三者扔进球场，或因被比赛无关的第三者妨碍而中断比赛时，是否重赛球必须由主裁判认定。

（3）双方同时发生失分的情况时（例如，一方运动员成功截击，在该球第二次落地的同时，该截击的运动员触网）。

（4）主裁判认为有必要重赛时。

注：比赛中球破损时，该分有效。

37. 暂停

比赛中允许暂停的情况如下：

（1）运动员由于伤病无法继续比赛，经主裁判认可时。此类暂停在一场比赛中，同一人最多只能两次，每次时间不可超过5分钟。

（2）主裁判认为有必要暂停时。

38. 禁止事项

（1）在比赛中禁止运动员接受搭档以外任何人的建议及身体上的帮助（但主裁判与裁判长讨论后认为必要时除外）。

（2）在比赛中，禁止任何非本场比赛的运动员、裁判员进入比赛场地，除非有特殊原因而被允许者。

39. 弃权

在比赛中有以下情况之一者，应判为弃权，对手赢得比赛，弃权的一方在比赛中所得的分数及局数仍然有效：

（1）已报名，但未能参加比赛的。

（2）经裁判长或竞赛委员会许可，运动员由于某些特殊原因要求弃权的。

（3）运动员由于伤病要求暂停，但未能在规定时间内恢复比赛判为暂停时间到，比赛结束（Time's up and game set）。

（4）运动员由于伤病要求弃权并经主裁判许可的。

（5）符合"竞赛组织"章节中第11条关于弃权的情况，无法再比赛时裁判长宣告比赛停止，比赛结束（Referee stop and game set）。

注：（1）比赛中因故无法再继续其余比赛，则判罚为弃权（所得分数、局数仍然有效）及取消比赛资格（之前的比赛成绩均取消并取消名次）。

（2）在团体赛出赛名单中，误将同一人姓名重复提交时，该重复名单及以后的各组视为弃权。

40. 禁止抗议的言行

（1）禁止运动员在比赛中抗议裁判员的的判罚，或不服判决而故意中断比赛。

（2）第40条第一款的规定，并非阻止运动员对裁判员的判定或处理事项提出质疑，但对于质疑，经裁判员给予解释说明后，则适用第一款的规定。

注：（1）禁止运动员故意利用异议，以达到改变比赛节奏的目的。

（2）运动员不能因要确认球的落点，而超越球网或球网的假定延长线；即使在自己的半场内，也不可靠近该落点。

（3）禁止运动员将球的落点擦拭掉；如果运动员擅自擦掉球印，可视为干扰（Interfere）而失分。

（4）对比赛有异议时，仅限于由该场运动员提出，对于分数的判定，只限于该分。

41. 警告

如运动员出现违反"竞赛规则"中第15条、第38条及第40条任何规定时，主裁判应对该运动员警告并出示黄牌（Yellow card）。

42. 取消比赛资格

（1）裁判长发现任何有违反竞赛规程的情况时，在与竞赛委员会协商后，可宣布取消该运动员的参赛资格。

（2）主裁判发现有下列情况之一者，宣布取消该运动员比赛资格，由对手获胜：

a. 接到大会出场比赛通知而仍不到场的运动员。

注：已通告比赛，运动员经过10分钟仍然拒不出场。

b. 如果一方运动员在一场比赛中，被主裁判警告达3次时，判罚红牌（Red card）。

注：在团体比赛开始后，发现未按照事先提交的出赛名单顺序出场时，则根据裁判规则第21条第（2）款b项处理，该球队失去比赛资格；但该团体赛比赛结束后才发现，则不适用本规定。

43. 申诉

（1）如果运动员对裁判员的判决、竞赛规则的解释或适用性认为有误时，根据规则该运动员可向裁判长提出申诉。

（2）对裁判长的裁决不得再次提出申诉。

（3）本场比赛结束且运动员互相行礼后，不能再提出申诉。

注：对于得失分有异议，如已经进入下一分的比赛时，不得再次提出；对于分数呼报错误，应在该局内提出，局数呼报错误的异议则应在比赛结束前提出。

44. 停止比赛与继续比赛

（1）由于天气和其他原因导致比赛中止或延期，当重新开始比赛时，应从中止当时最后的比分继续比赛。

（2）若更改场地或延期比赛，其后比赛场区的选择，应由原来选场区者选择；假如是在同日同一球场继续比赛时，则应从比赛停止时相同的位置继续比赛。

45. 规则上的疑义

如在比赛中出现规则中没有说明的问题，主裁判征求裁判长的意见后进行判定。

单打比赛

1. 目的

为保障软式网球比赛（单打比赛）的进行，特制定所必须遵守的事项。除单打比赛所制定的事项外，双打比赛的各项规则均适用于单打比赛（图2-7）。

图2-7　软式网球单打比赛

2. 球场

单打场地是将球网两边发球区的边线延长至底线，作为单打球场的边线，两边线之间所截取的端线部分为底线，场地长为23.77米，宽为8.23米。

3. 界线名称及长度

球场的区域、界线名称及长度（图2-8）：

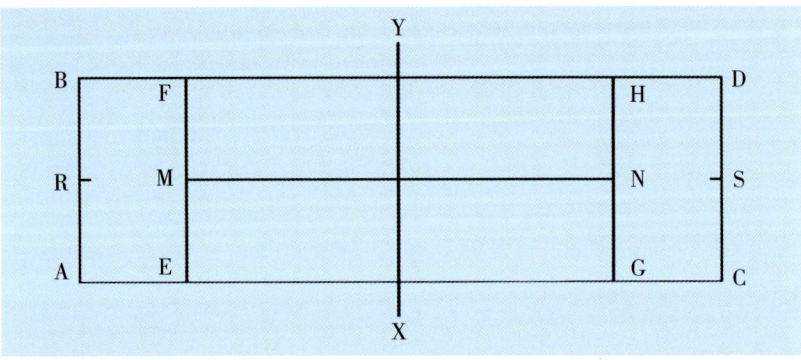

界线名称	符号	长度
边线	A-C、B-D	23.77米
底线	A-B、C-D	8.23米
发球边线	E-G、F-H	12.80米
发球线	E-F、G-H	8.23米
发球中线	M-N	12.80米
中点标志	R、S	0.15米

图2-8　软式网球单打场地平面图

4. 发球与接球

（1）除决胜局外，双方轮流发球，各发一局。发球时应从右发球区开始，发向对角的发球区，得分或失分后再换到左发球区，以此顺序交替进行，另一方运动员则接发球。

（2）决胜局，双方运动员的发球每两分轮换，按照发球顺序，所轮及的运动员开始发球，另一方运动员接发球。

5. 比赛局数

单打比赛一般以七局四胜制为原则进行。

第三章 裁判规则

第一节 总则

1. 目的

本规定旨在明确软式网球赛事中裁判工作的相关事项。

图3-1 2016年中国杯国际软式网球锦标赛技术官员

第二节 裁判团

2. 裁判团

（1）赛事裁判团由裁判长和裁判员组成。
注：裁判长与裁判员各行其责，以不兼职为原则。

（2）裁判长团队可由1～5人组成，其中一人为首席裁判长，负责领导、监督其他裁判长及裁判员。

（3）比赛中，每片场地上的裁判员原则上应由4人组成，但是在有参赛运动员参与裁判工作的情况下，裁判组可减少专职裁判人数。

（4）根据比赛需要，主办方可在每片场地安排1名赛场监督。

3. 裁判长

裁判长除了必须给裁判员指导和建议外，当裁判员在比赛中的判定与规则的解释运用被运动员认为有错误而提出申诉或质疑时，应充分了解其内容后做出判定。

4. 场地监督

场地监督应负责所管场地的比赛顺利进行，并在有需要时给予裁判员指示和建议。

5. 裁判员

原则上每场比赛应安排一名主裁判与一名副裁判员，但根据实际情况，可以不安排副裁判员。如果需要，可以再安排两名司线员。

6. 裁判员的任务

（1）裁判员为保障比赛的顺利进行，必须依照竞赛规则进行公正且迅速的判罚。

（2）比赛进行中，主裁判在裁判椅上掌握比赛进度的同时，不仅对自己的责任区域做出判罚，还要对其他裁判员的判罚手势及宣告确认后，做出清晰的宣告，并记录于计分表。

（3）副裁判员及司线员按照"裁判规则"第9条的（2）和（3）款所指定的位置，对其所负责的区域进行判罚并协助主裁判。

（4）副裁判员及司线员对他们所负责的区域的判罚以手势告知主裁判，其他职责的判定，以手势配合宣告的形式告知主裁判。

（5）副裁判员除了管理比赛用球外，还负责调整比赛用球的弹跳高度。

第三节 裁判员的职责

7. 裁判员须知

裁判员为了使比赛能够公正且顺利地进行,务必熟知下列事项:
(1)应熟悉竞赛规则及裁判规则,并能准确运用。
(2)在执行裁判工作时,除比赛主办方指定服装外,应穿着软式网球裁判服装。
(3)在执行裁判工作时,应遵守下列事项:

a.裁判员应在运动员出场前在自己负责的场地提前做好准备,若有必要应催促运动员及时进入场地。

b.裁判员应语言、举止得当。

c.裁判员应努力保障比赛公正、顺利进行。

d.裁判员应公正、及时地做出判罚决定。

e.裁判员应按"裁判规则"第10条的规定,大声、清晰地宣告判罚。

f.裁判员应按"裁判规则"第11条规定,做出清晰、正确的判罚手势。

g.裁判员应和同场其他裁判员保持良好的合作关系。

h.裁判员不应越权判罚同场其他裁判员所负责判罚的区域。

8. 裁判员的责任区域

裁判员责任区域及职责划分如下:
(1)各裁判员责任区域的划分(图3-2):

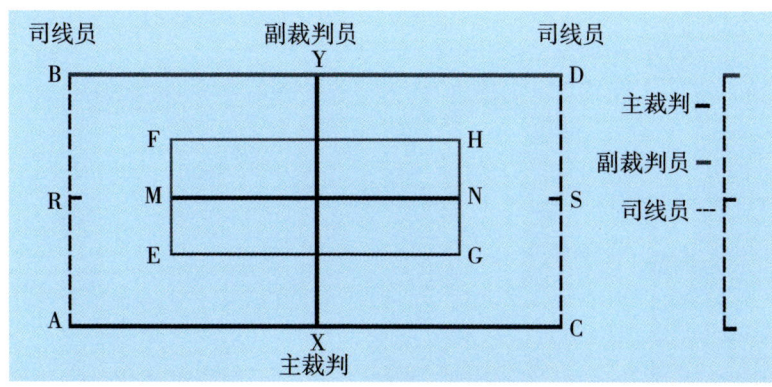

图3-2

a.主裁判责任区域：A—C、E—G、M—N、X—Y

b.副裁判员责任区域：B—D、F—H、E—F、G—H、X—Y

c.司线员责任区域：A—B、 C—D

（2）其他职责：

a.主裁判职责：两跳、连击、持球、直接球、干扰、触身球、触及、擦拍球、过网击球、触网、穿网、重发球、重赛球、脚误。

b.副裁判员职责：同主裁判。

c.司线员职责：脚误、直接球、触身、擦拍球。

（3）若出现副裁判员和司线员空缺的情况，他们执裁区域和司线应由主裁判来判罚。

9. 裁判员位置

比赛中裁判员的位置如下：

（1）主裁判应坐在裁判员座椅上（图3-3）。

图3-3

（2）副裁判员应位于主裁判对面的边线外，离开网柱0.6米处。当判定发球时，应迅速移动到接球方发球线的假定延长线上，且不得进入场地内。判定发球结束后,应迅速回到原来位置,继续判定比赛(图3-4)。

图3-4

(3)司线员坐在位于底线的假定延长线上,且离边线的距离不少于5米的主裁判对面的椅子上(图3-5)。

图3-5

10. 宣告

（1）判定及胜负分数的宣告，依照"裁判术语"。

（2）得分及局数的比分，应由主裁判宣告，先报发球方的比分。

（3）暂停后要继续比赛时，主裁判应大声宣告"暂停时间到"（No time）。

注：当主裁判宣告比分错误后，裁判员及运动员均未发现继续进行比赛，此时即使有人发现错误，也不得中断比赛。在第一次发球失误时，或在下一分发球宣告时，宣告"更正"（Correction），再宣告正确的比分。

11. 手势

比赛中裁判员手势和身体姿势应按如下所示：

（1）界内球时裁判员原则上不做手势，但运动员无法确定球是否为界内或界外时，可做界内球手势，以单手伸直向正前斜下方，手掌心向下。

（2）主裁判原则上不做手势，若有必要时，可以做出与副裁判员一样的手势。

（3）副裁判员的手势及身体姿势要求如下图所示：

a. 发球判定手势，副裁判员应站在预备位置，如图3-6A所示，以一脚（接球方这边的脚）向前踏步，膝关节微屈，同侧的一手轻放膝关节上，另一手则放置背后腰部，其手掌心向上。

图3-6A 发球线判定

发球失误手势（发球未过网除外）如图3-6B所示，脚向前踏步，手指伸直并拢，肘部弯曲成直角上举（在预备位置的脚向前踏步，出同侧的手）；重发球手势，如图3-6C、图3-6D所示，以直立姿势手臂垂直上举（在预备位置的脚向前踏步，出同侧的手），将食指与中指伸直（第一次发球）或将食指伸直（第二次发球）并同时宣告"重发"（Let）。

图3-6B　发球失误　　　　图3-6C　重发球　　　　图3-6D　重发球
　　　　　　　　　　　　（同时宣告）　　　　　　（同时宣告）

　　b. 界外球手势如图3-6E所示，正视球的落地点直立，然后上举单臂，手指伸直掌心向内。

　　c. 其他职责失分手势如图3-6F所示，伸出单臂用食指指向该运动员，并宣告失分名称。

图3-6E　界外球　　　　　　　　图3-6F　其他职责
　　　　　　　　　　　　　　　　（同时宣告）

　　d. 重赛球手势如图3-6G所示，前臂双举、双手于脸部前交叉摆动几次，同时宣告"重赛球"（No count）。

图3-6G　重赛球（同时宣告）

e.暂停手势如图3-6H所示，面对主裁判上举双臂直立，掌心向主裁判，同时宣告"暂停"（Time）。

注：界内球原则上不做手势，但有必要向主裁判示意时，如图3-6I所示。

图3-6H　暂停（同时宣告）　　　图3-6I　界内球（原则上不做手势，
　　　　　　　　　　　　　　　　　　　　但有必要时可以做手势）

（4）司线员的手势应与副裁判员手势相同。

注：1）比赛中的判定，对于责任区域部分，主裁判、副裁判员（司线员）应宣告或以手势告之，而对于其他职责部分的各项规定，裁判员以手指指向该失分的运动员，并附加宣告。

2）副裁判员在判定接发球后，应迅速移位至原来位置，距离网柱后方0.6米处站立，观察比赛的进行（图3-6J、图3-6K）。

图3-6J　副裁判员站姿（位于主裁判对面边线外，离网柱0.6米处）

图3-6K　司线员站姿（位于底线假设延长线外）

3）对于图3-6F其他职责的失分，指向该失分运动员的手，是以球网为准，球网左侧的用左手，球网右侧的用右手。

12. 球点的确认

裁判员对自己责任区域的球的落点，不能确定是界内球或界外球时，可以查看球的落点后再做出决定。如果是主裁判的责任区，可以委派副裁判员查看，如副裁判员不能确定，主裁判可以离开裁判椅亲自确认落点后再做判断。

13. 判定的协调

裁判员对自己责任区内的判定无法作出正确判断时，可以征求其他裁判员的意见后再做判定。

注：裁判员的判定，按照裁判规则第8条的规定虽然各有各的责任区，但在比赛中，由于运动员的移动或其他因素的影响而无法确定球的落点时，裁判员之间可以用小手势或眼神进行示意，相互配合。

14. 最终判定

比赛时,如果运动员对裁判员的判决有疑问,裁判员应对其疑问内容了解确定后,由主裁判做出最终的判定并告知运动员。如再有异议,依照竞赛规则第41条、第42条的规定处理。

注:(1)依据竞赛规则第40条,虽然不允许运动员向裁判员提出抗议,但运动员对判罚结果有疑问而提出质疑时,就其质疑内容了解清楚后,如果判定确实有误,应予以更正。

(2)对于分数的错误,应在该局内;对于局数的错误则应在该场比赛结束前重新判定。

15. 改判

裁判员的判定如有明显的错误,主裁判可以改判,但只限于该分。

16. 中止比赛

比赛中裁判员因判定错误,且做出宣告或手势而导致比赛中断,主裁判应立即停止比赛。如果主裁判错误判罚的宣告或手势影响到比赛的进行,这两种情况均应判定为重赛球(未完成接球时是重发球)。如该宣告或手势并未影响到比赛的进行,应立即更正其判定。

17. 计分错误

裁判员在宣告分数、局数有错误时,应在第一次发球失误后,或进入下一分开始前宣告"更正"(correction),然后再宣告正确的分数或局数。如果在比赛进行中发现分数、局数错误,则不可中断比赛,且该分有效。

18. 弃权

运动员在比赛中被发现有下列情况时,则被判定为弃权,宣布对方获胜。负的一方所得分数及局数仍然有效:

(1)报名后不出场参加比赛。

(2)运动员因故申请退出比赛,经裁判长或竞赛委员会同意。

（3）比赛时运动员因受伤被允许暂停，但在规定时间内无法恢复比赛。

（4）运动员在比赛中由于身体不适或受伤不能继续比赛而要求弃权，经主裁判认可。

（5）出现"竞赛组织"章节中第11条无法继续比赛的情况。

19. 口头警告

如果运动员、教练员、球队等相关人员影响了比赛的正常进行，主裁判可以给予其口头警告。

注：如果场外的观众对比赛的顺利进行产生了影响，虽然可以给予口头警告，但不能以第20条的正式警告方式处理，如有必要可以报告给裁判长。裁判长认为对比赛产生了不良影响时，有权警告或命令该观众退场。

20. 正式警告

主裁判认为运动员明显地违反"竞赛规则"第15条、第38及第40条时，依照竞赛规则第41条可正式警告黄牌（Yellow card）。

注：比赛中，运动员、领队、教练员或该球队的加油声，虽然能使比赛气氛激烈、高涨，但过度激烈时，反而变成不愉快的动作行为。如裁判员认为对比赛有不良影响时，则适用口头警告或正式警告。

21. 取消比赛资格

（1）裁判长发现运动员或球队有违反大会竞赛规程的行为时，应与竞赛委员会协商后，宣布取消该运动员或球队的比赛资格。

（2）当主裁判遇有以下情况，报告裁判长并允许后，可取消该队运动员或该队的比赛资格，并宣布对方获胜：

a. 运动员被通知上场比赛而仍不出场进行比赛时；

b. 在团体赛中不按照事先提交的上场比赛名单顺序出场；

c. 一场比赛中同一组运动员被警告达3次判罚红牌（Red card）时（图3-7）。

图3-7　比赛中使用的红黄牌

22. 禁止更换裁判员

比赛中不允许更换裁判员，除非出现以下情况：
（1）由于身体原因无法继续履行裁判员职责时。
（2）运动员兼裁判员而影响比赛时。

第四节　比赛进程

23. 裁判工作程序

裁判员执行比赛进行的程序如下：
（1）双方运动员面对球网站立于各自发球线后中央位置，与此同时，主裁判和副裁判员站在边线外侧裁判椅前，司线员应分别站在主裁判、副裁判员身边，以球网相隔，分开站立（图3-8）。

图3-8

（2）按照上述规定，队员们应根据主裁判的手势走向球网，同时，裁判员应沿着球网走向发球中线附近（图3-9）。

图3-9

（3）在球网前，双方运动员首先互相行礼，然后向裁判员行礼（图3-10）。

图3-10

（4）主裁判确认双方运动员身份（图3-11）。

图3-11

（5）在团体赛中，双方所有运动员应面对球网分别排队站在各自底线后，按照主裁判的手势，两队走向网边相互行礼。如果球队领队在场，其位置应靠近裁判员。球队行礼结束后，根据单项比赛规定，逐一进行比赛流程（图3-12）。

图3-12

（6）比赛开始前，副裁判员或主裁判（如果无副裁判员时）向双方参赛选手出示一枚硬币的A、B面，然后把硬币抛向空中，如果落下后是A面，在主裁判右边的选手获得选择权；如果落下后是B面，在主裁判左边的选手则获得选择权。获得选择权的选手可以选择发球/接发球或场地中的任何一项，对方选手可以在剩下的项目中进行选择（为了比赛的顺利进行，这项工作亦可赛前在场外进行，图3-13）。

图3-13

（7）如果比赛球采用选择制时，由得到优先选择权的运动员选择，但团体赛时用双方代表所选择的球进行比赛。

（8）挑边结束后，运动员开始赛前热身练习，裁判员回到各自的指定位置。热身练习一般不超过1分钟，但裁判长与竞赛委员会协商后可以减少或省略准备活动的时间。决定一经做出，立即通知裁判员。

（9）热身练习时间结束后，主裁判宣告"准备"（Ready），双方运动员各就位准备开始比赛。

（10）当双方运动员就位后，主裁判宣告"发球方××先生/女士来自××，接球方××先生/女士来自××，比赛采用×局制，比赛开始"（Service side, Mr./Ms. ------- from ----- and Mr./Ms. ------ from -----, Receive side，Mr./Ms.――――― from ――――― and Mr./Ms.――――――― from ―――――，Seven/Nine game match，play ball）。

（11）从比赛开始到结束，主裁判必须依照竞赛规则、裁判规则的规定执行，确保比赛正确且圆满地进行。

（12）当比赛结束时，主裁判宣告"比赛结束"（Game set）后，应即刻走下裁判员座椅，并要求运动员们走到网前的同时与其他裁判员一起沿着球网走到场地中间。主裁判宣告比赛结果"比分×比×，××获胜"（This match to Mr./Ms.―――――― and Mr./Ms.――――――，with the score × to ×）。然后，双方运动员先相互行礼，再与裁判员行礼，最后退场（图3–14）。

图3–14

（13）在团体赛中，所有比赛结束后，双方全体运动员站在各自底线时，在主裁判示意后走到网前，主裁判宣告比赛结果"比分×比×，××（队名）获胜"（This competition to ―――――――，with the score × to ×）。然后，双方运动员先相互行礼，再与裁判员行礼，最后退场。

24. 计分表

计分表原则上采用规定样式，依照记录要领由主裁判填写，但从宣告比赛结束到互相行礼之间，主裁判没有足够的时间填写各记录栏时，可等到互相行礼后，再尽快完成。

计分表填写要求：

（1）主裁判应准确填写计分表。组别、场号、场次、运动员姓名等栏信息原则上由工作人员事先填写，主裁判应予以确认，并负责填上裁判员的姓名。

（2）当发球方、接球方已经确定后，应在比数栏中，每一局的S（发球方）及R（接球方）处画圈。

（3）每一局计分栏中，得分时画"○"，失分时画"×"，由左至右双方同时记录。

（4）每一局比赛结束时，双方的得分数应记录于得分比数栏，在胜者得分处画圈。

（5）比赛结束时，双方的局数应记录于局数栏，在胜者局数处画圈。

（6）对运动员提出警告时，应在警告栏中的Y（黄牌）或R（红牌）处画圈，并将警告内容记于下方备注栏处，在团体赛中，对领队或教练员的警告也填写于此栏。

（7）运动员由于身体原因出现的暂停，应在暂停栏5（分钟）处画圈。

第四章 竞赛组织

第一节 总则

1. 目的

（1）本规则旨在规定软式网球比赛运营所需的必要事项。

（2）大赛的主办/承办单位原则上应依照本规则组织比赛。

2. 竞赛规程

比赛的主办/承办单位必须制定竞赛规程并通知参加者，竞赛规程的内容原则上应包括以下内容：

（1）比赛名称。

（2）主办单位名称。

（3）承办单位名称。

（4）协办单位名称。

（5）比赛日期。

（6）比赛地点。

（7）比赛球场名称。

（8）比赛项目。

（9）比赛日程安排。

（10）参赛资格。

（11）报名方法。

（12）比赛规则及补充说明。

（13）比赛方法及名次排定。

（14）抽签办法。

（15）参赛条件。

（16）比赛相关设备及用球。

（17）兴奋剂检测。

（18）医疗护理。

（19）安保管理。

（20）奖励办法。

（21）参赛费用。

（22）领队会议。

第二节 比赛场地设施

3. 场地设施

比赛场地原则上应包括以下设施：

（1）比赛场地的设施包括软式网球场地、固定设备（网、网柱及裁判椅）和附属设施（挡网、运动员休息椅、记分板、观众席、洗手间、运动员等候室、更衣室、竞赛官员席、贵宾席、记者席、医务人员席、场地刷、线刷、淋浴间、旗杆、饮水设备等）。

（2）在若干场地中应有一个作为主赛场，该主赛场与其他场地相对独立并设有观众席较为妥当。

（3）球场及球场的界外空地表面、室外应为黏土、人工沙地及草地或全天候型化学材质场地，而室内应以木板、硬质橡胶或化学材质等为表面，并将场地情况写明于竞赛规程中。

（4）根据比赛规模，必须有足够数量的场地，确保在赛期内完成全部比赛。

（5）运动员休息席须设在球场界外空地，并保证不会对比赛造成干扰。

第三节　竞赛事宜

4. 竞赛项目

竞赛项目由主办/承办单位在下列项目中决定，并在竞赛规程中写明：
（1）男子双打、女子双打。
（2）男子单打、女子单打。
（3）混合双打。
（4）男子团体、女子团体。

5. 竞赛日程

竞赛日程安排由主办/承办单位决定后，写明于竞赛规程中。

6. 报名资格

运动员的报名资格由主办/承办单位决定后，写明于竞赛规程中。

7. 报名方法

（1）报名方法由主办/承办单位决定后，写明于竞赛规程中。
（2）报名日期截止后原则上不得再更改，但经主办/承办单位批准的除外。在这种情况下，管理机构应在竞赛规程中对此做出澄清。

8. 适用于本规则的特殊情况

比赛原则上按《软式网球竞赛手册》中"竞赛规则"和"裁判规则"执行。主办/承办单位也可以按下列规定提出比赛采用的规则、特殊补充及竞赛规则以外的规定或说明，但是在这种情况下，管理机构应在竞赛规程中明确说明。

例如：
（1）各国如有国内使用的规则，在国内比赛时可使用该"国内规则"。

（2）团体赛时各球队设教练员、领队各一人，在这种情况下，教练员、领队也可以作为运动员参赛。

（3）团体赛时运动员可进入规定休息席，在竞赛规则认可范围内助威加油或协助场上运动员。

9. 竞赛制度

（1）竞赛制度原则上依照下列各项进行，由主办/承办单位决定后，编入竞赛规程中。

a. 淘汰制（淘汰制的最终获胜者为第一名，其他名次的确定方法，依次排序）。

b. 循环制（所有参赛选手都有机会相遇，排名方法由积分决定）。

c. 淘汰、循环混合制（根据比赛规模，酌情采用上述两种方法）。

（2）团体赛的比赛方法如下：

a. 团体赛不管是淘汰制或循环制，两队事先按规定奇数场次的相同次序名单按顺序进行比赛，胜场数多的球队获胜，比赛形式包括单打、双打或单双打混合赛，原则上必须全部组数赛完。但主办/承办单位可决定：a) 按照出场次序名单进行比赛，先胜半数以上场次的球队获胜，剩下的比赛不必进行；b) 由于比赛需要，两场以上的比赛分别在不同的场地同时进行时，不管比赛的次序如何，先赢得半数胜场的球队获胜。

b. 在运动员人数不足的情况下，如果该队可以参加半数以上的比赛，并且在裁判长和竞赛组织官员同意的情况下，可以参加比赛。比赛按预先提交的顺序进行，由于人数不足而无法参加的比赛按弃权处理。

c. 一场比赛的局数由举办/承办单位决定，并在竞赛规程上写明。

10. 循环赛中名次的判定

循环赛中的排名由以下几种方法决定：

（1）两队胜率相同时，两队相互间比赛胜者名次列前。

（2）3个或3个以上的队积分相同时，将仅看这几支相关联的队伍之间的比赛的结果，胜率高者名次列前。

（3）依照以上方法仍无法决定名次时，积分相同的队伍之间的排名以该相关队伍之间的比赛结果按下列顺序决定：a.（总胜场数）-（总负场数）之差，数值大者名次列前；如相等则以b.（总胜局数）-（总负局数）之差，数值大者名次列前；如相等则以c.（总得分数）-（总失分数）之差，数值大者名次列前。不论哪步结果出来，一旦仅有两个队数值相同，则可看两者之间的胜负关系，胜者名次靠前。

（4）如果以上方式仍无法决定名次时，由主办/承办单位采用抽签或适当方法决定。

11. 循环赛中弃权的处理办法

在循环制比赛中，如果有选手未完成比赛就选择弃权，除赛事举办/承办单位另有规定外，应按以下办法处理：

（1）团体赛中，一队运动员不足半数时，不得继续比赛。已参加的比赛所得成绩判定为无效，但符合竞赛规则第39条及裁判规则第18条而弃权时，则已取得的成绩有效。

（2）因缺少运动员未达到球队的半数时，经裁判长及竞赛委员会同意，可以继续进行比赛；但因弃权而不能进行的比赛则判为零分。

（3）单项赛运动员在全部比赛没有结束之前，中途退出比赛，其已比赛成绩均判定为无效，以零分处理。但符合竞赛规则第39条及裁判规则第18条而弃权时，则已取得的成绩有效。

（4）在全部比赛的过程中，一时无法继续比赛，经裁判长及竞赛委员会同意，可以继续进行比赛，没有参加的比赛均以零分处理。

12. 弃权

适用于竞赛规则第39条及裁判规则第18条的弃权行为时，判对方赢得比赛，负方运动员在此前所得分数及局数仍然有效。

13. 取消资格

（1）如有竞赛规则第42条及裁判规则第21条的情况发生时，取消运动员参赛资格，且此前所取得的成绩均被取消。

（2）在团体赛中，如某队发生取消资格条款中的行为，该队将被取消比赛资格。

（3）在淘汰制比赛中，被取消资格的单打、双打、团体队伍所击败的单打、双打、团体队伍，不能继续比赛。

14. 赛程编排

赛程编排由主办/承办单位根据下列原则公平进行。

（1）单淘汰制：

a. 参赛人数刚好是2的n次方，如4、8、16、32、64、128、256、512，抽签和种子选手的安排如下：

16人淘汰赛（其他2的n次方的数字排列方法相同）编排范例如图4-1所示。

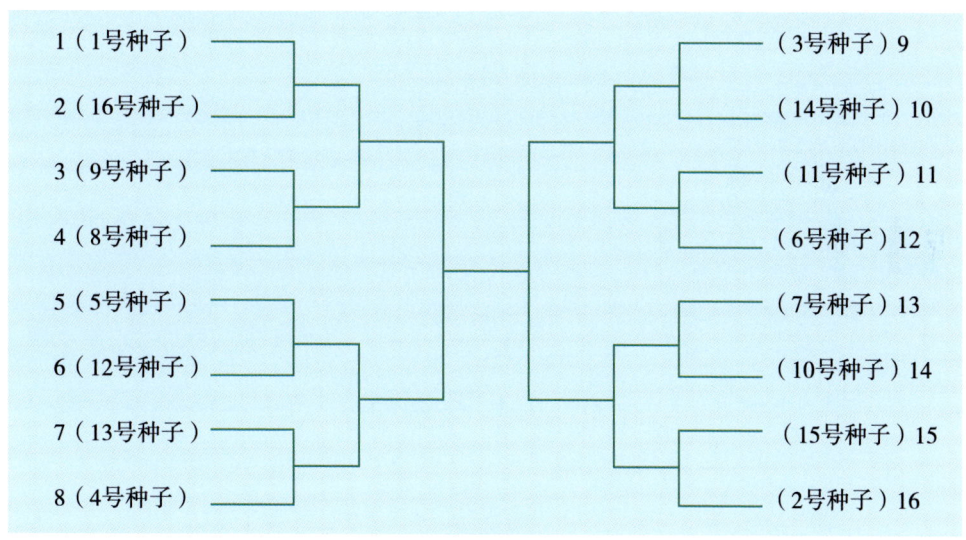

图4-1

b. 如果参赛人数不是2的n次方，则取大于且最接近参赛人数的2的n次方的数做基数。基数减去参赛人数为轮空数，参赛人数减去轮空数则是第一轮要参加比赛的运动员人数。在比赛的签位表中，把运动员分成2、4或8区，一个区中单位数为奇数时，种子顺位较高者编排入该区，一个区中单位数为3时，则种子排名靠前的选手轮空。

9人淘汰赛编排范例如图4-2所示。

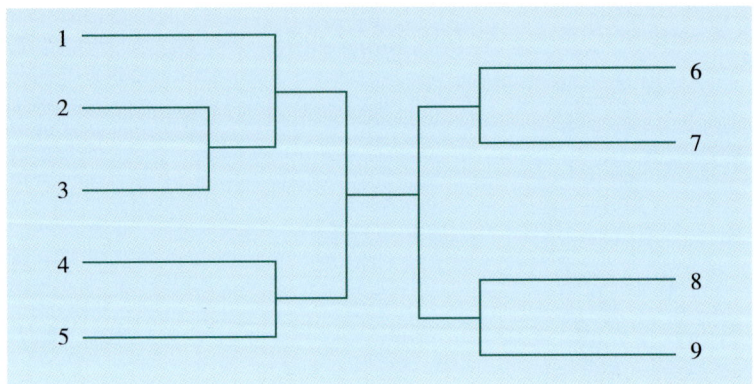

图4-2

11人淘汰赛编排范例如图4-3所示。

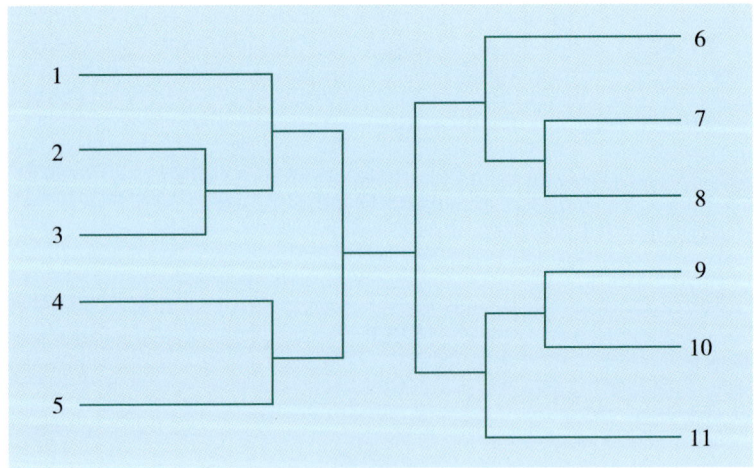

图4-3

（2）循环制：

a. 根据参赛人数将运动员分成两组或两组以上。

b. 参赛选手的签位及种子选手的位置按照单淘汰制方式进行编排，根据参赛人数分成合适的组数。

如有16名参赛运动员，则将其分成4组，种子选手安排如下：

第一组	1	16	9	8
第二组	4	13	12	5
第三组	3	14	11	6
第四组	2	15	10	7

c. 循环赛的比赛顺序

3名运动员每组1-2，2-3，1-3
4名运动员每组1-2，3-4，1-3，2-4，2-3，1-4
5名运动员每组1-2，3-4，2-5，1-3，4-5，2-3，1-4，3-5，2-4，1-5
6名运动员每组1-2，3-4，5-6，1-3，2-5，4-6，3-5，2-6，1-4，3-6，2-4，1-5，2-3，4-5，1-6

如以上比赛顺序需要调整，由主办/承办单位决定。
如同一组中有来自相同单位的运动员时，必须先进行他们之间的比赛。

15. 比赛成绩的记录

主办/承办单位必须用以下方法将比赛成绩记录下来：

（1）单项赛需记录局比分。
（2）团体赛需记录场分。
（3）弃权（Retirement）时，用"R"标记，并记录其有效分数。
（4）取消比赛资格（Disqualification）时，用"D"标记，淘汰赛当场比赛记"D"，循环赛所有比赛都要标记"D"。
（5）比赛结束后，如果运动员、配对搭档或队伍有变动，必须更正过来。

16. 参赛资格

所有参赛运动员必须遵守主办/承办单位及竞赛规程所规定的参赛资格。

17. 比赛用球

比赛用球由主办/承办单位写明于竞赛规程中。

18. 兴奋剂检测

如果需要在比赛中实施兴奋剂检测，应在竞赛规程中通知参赛者，参赛者应按照竞赛规程的规定进行兴奋剂检测。

19. 医疗监护

主办/承办单位在比赛期间，应注意运动员及有关人员的健康及临时发生的事故，必须有充分的准备及应急措施。

20. 奖励办法

主办/承办单位须在竞赛规程中告知具体的奖励办法。

21. 参赛经费

如需向参赛者收取费用时，应在竞赛规程中详细说明。

22. 领队会议

为了实现比赛的顺利进行，在比赛前需召开领队会议，主办/承办单位应在竞赛规程中写明会议的时间、日期、目的和需要参加的人员等。

23. 竞赛官员

竞赛官员应由主办/承办单位组织，以实现比赛的顺利进行。

24. 裁判团

（1）裁判团分为裁判长和裁判员，由主办/承办单位组织聘请。

（2）裁判长应指导裁判员进行公正的判罚，并对比赛规则和裁判规则及其适用范围做出适当的解释。

（3）裁判长有两人以上时，其中一人为首席裁判长。

（4）正式比赛中，每场比赛的裁判员原则上由一名主裁判、一名副裁判员及两名司线员组成，但主办/承办单位决定不设副裁判员、司线员或由参赛选手担任裁判员时，可减少裁判员人数。

（5）如有需要可以增设赛场监督。

25. 安全保障

主办/承办单位为保障比赛顺利进行及便于管理，可根据需要为运动员、官员及其他相关人员制作并发放ID卡。

26. 入场费

主办/承办单位允许收取入场费。

27. 赞助商

主办/承办单位应允许有赞助商，赞助商的有关事宜由主办/承办单位决定。

注：竞赛组织工作补充说明：

1. 软式网球比赛器材还需记分牌、秒表、挂钟、地毯及领奖台、量网器等。

2. 比赛名称

根据总任务确定比赛名称，名称要显示比赛的性质、年份及届数。赛会期间的文件、会标、宣传材料等方面的名称要统一。

3. 比赛目的

根据举行本次比赛活动的总要求，简要说明本次比赛的目的和任务。如为了进一步贯彻落实全民健身计划，增强学生整体素质；普及体育运动，增强人民体质；提高软式网球运动水平；总结教练教学训练工作经验，增进团结促进友谊等。

4. 比赛时间、地点和主办单位、承办单位、协办单位

比赛时间应写清楚预算、决赛开始/结束的年、月、日；举办比赛的地点和举办竞赛的单位（包括主办、承办以及协办单位）。

5. 比赛项目和组别

举办比赛所设置的竞赛项目，单项比赛规程写明各组别的各竞赛小项目。

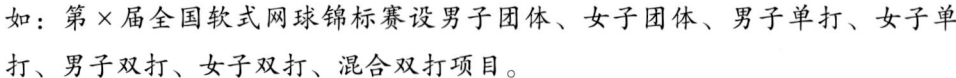

如：第×届全国软式网球锦标赛设男子团体、女子团体、男子单打、女子单打、男子双打、女子双打、混合双打项目。

6. 参赛单位和各单位参赛人数

按有关规定，依次写明参加比赛的每个单位，以及各单位男女运动员、领队、教练员及工作人员人数。每名运动员可参加的项目数，每项比赛限报人数，以及参赛的其他有关规定。

7. 运动员资格

运动员资格是指参赛运动员的条件或标准，包括运动员年龄、健康状况、代表资格、运动等级、运动成绩、达标规定等。

8. 竞赛办法

确定比赛所采取的竞赛办法，如淘汰法、循环法、混合法及其他特殊的方法。比赛是否分阶段进行，各阶段采用的竞赛方法是否相同，各阶段比赛的成绩如何计算和衔接。

9. 竞赛规则

明确有无制定其他规则（根据实际情况）。

10. 录取名次与具体奖励办法

（1）规定竞赛录取的名次，奖励优胜者的名次及办法。如对优胜者分别给予奖杯、奖旗、奖状、奖章及奖金等。

（2）设置体育道德风尚奖的奖励办法等。

11. 报名办法

规定各单位运动员（队）报名的人数、时间和截止日期，书面报名的格式和投寄的地点，并应注明以寄出或寄到的邮戳日期为准，以及违反报名规定的处理办法。

12. 抽签日期和地点

明确具体的抽签日期和地点。

13. 兴奋剂检测

举办/承办单位须说明兴奋剂检测所用的仪器，运动员必须根据竞赛规则的条款进行兴奋剂检测。

14. 其他事项

（1）有关未尽事宜需补充说明，如经费、交通、食宿条件等。

（2）注明规程解释权归属单位。

15. 比赛具体工作安排

（1）赛前工作安排

①确定组委会名单。

②确定代表队名单。

③竞赛日程。

④场地安排及示意图。

⑤开、闭幕式的策划与安排。

⑥资格审查。

⑦报名汇总。

⑧抽签、编排。

⑨印制秩序册及有关表格。

⑩落实场地器材。

⑪裁判员学习、实习。

⑫召开有关会议。

⑬赛事指南的准备与发放。

⑭入口处的接待。

⑮比赛用球的确定和所需比赛用球数量的保证。

⑯所需助理人员数量的保障及其任务的安排。

⑰运动员号码布的准备与管理。

⑱其他。

（2）比赛期间工作

①记录、公布比赛成绩。

②检查和管理场地器材与设施。

③遇到特殊情况需要更改比赛场地、日期、时间等，要及时通知各队。

④合理安排裁判员，及时组织裁判员会议进行总结，从而改进工作，保证比赛顺利进行。

⑤仲裁负责受理申诉、抗议等，保证比赛正常进行。

（3）赛后工作

①及时将比赛成绩、名次交由裁判长宣布。

②召开竞赛委员会会议，听取工作汇报及意见，决定体育道德风尚奖的评选结果。

③组织颁奖仪式，印发成绩册，安排和办理各队及裁判员离会有关事宜。

④完成赛会总结并向主管部门汇报。

第16届世界软式网球锦标赛开幕式

第16届世界软式网球锦标赛中国队合影

第五章 软式网球信任制比赛裁判方法

在软式网球赛事中,有些比赛可能初赛阶段参赛队员较多,或者赛事级别较低,没有安排主裁判,比赛采用信任制,因此特别制定了运动员参加信任制比赛的一些程序,以此保证赛事公平、公正、顺利进行。

当然,在这些比赛中会出现很多问题,所以裁判员应尽可能多地在球场边走动,巡查,观察比赛的进行。运动员在遇到问题时能尽快地找到裁判员,裁判员在遇到不同情况时,应用以下程序处理。

1. 信任制比赛巡场裁判员工作程序

(1)近线球的争议

如果裁判员被叫到场上处理一个近线球的争议,而且裁判员并没有观看这一分的比赛,应该询问谁对这个球做的呼报(球落在他自己这侧场地),并且对这个呼报是否确定。如果该运动员对这个呼报十分确定,则维持其原来的呼报。

在有球印的情况下:

如果运动员对其对手的呼报有疑惑,他能要求对手指出球印;

如果运动员擦掉球印,则他认可这个呼报;

如果对球印有争议,可以呼叫巡场裁判员做出决定;

巡场裁判员首先应该跟运动员确认是否同意这个球印,再来解读球印;

如果运动员认可这个球印,只是对球印的解读结果有争议,巡场裁判员将通过对球印的判断来决定是界内球还是界外球,如果还是不能判断,则将维持最初运动员对该球的呼报。

如果运动员的争议是两个不同落点的球印,裁判员应询问击球的性质及方向,这些信息可能帮助确定正确的球印。如果还是不能确定,则将维持最初运动员对该球的呼报。

如有近线球问题的出现，为了确保比赛的顺利进行，应设法安排一位主裁判承担该场比赛的裁判工作，负责所有的呼报，如果不能安排主裁判进行执裁，也可让巡场裁判员留在场上观看剩下的比赛，并且告诉运动员，他将纠正场上任何运动员做出的明显错误呼报，而且将直接判罚失分。如有必要，将由在场裁判员检查球印。

（2）其他呼报

当出现有关重赛、两跳、击球失误的争议时，巡场裁判员应尽量向运动员了解清楚到底发生了什么、具体的情况和做出这个呼报的依据，然后再做出合适的决定。

脚误只能由巡场裁判员呼报，而不是对手。但是，只有在场上的当职裁判员才可以呼报脚误。场外的裁判员不能做出脚误的呼报。

（3）明显错误的呼报

如果巡场裁判员在场外观看比赛，发现一名运动员做出了明显错误的呼报，他可以到场上告诉这名运动员，这个错误的呼报是对对手的一次无意干扰，要重赛这一分。并且还要告诉该名运动员如再做出明显的错误呼报，将被认为是故意干扰并且失分，如有必要，还可以同时给予一个正式警告。但巡场裁判员在给予正式警告前必须确信被罚运动员所做出的是一个故意的、恶劣的错误呼报。

2. 信任制比赛运动员须知

当运动员进行的是信任制比赛时，必须遵守以下基本原则：

（1）每名运动员负责其自己这侧半场球网的所有球的呼报。

（2）所有"Out""Fault"的呼报，应在球落地后以迅速、大声的确保能让对手听见的声音喊出。

（3）如果不确定，运动员必须做出有利于对手的呼报。

（4）如果一名运动员错误地呼报了"Out"，然后马上意识到这是一个好球，这一分应该重赛。除非在此前的比赛中该运动员已经有一次错误的"Out"

呼报，在这种情况下呼报的运动员失分。

（5）每次一发前，发球运动员要用足够大确保对手能听到的声音呼报比分。

（6）如果一名运动员对对手的行为或呼报不满意，应叫裁判长或巡场裁判员到场。

运动员如果不能公平地遵守信任制的比赛程序，裁判长及巡场裁判员可以给予正式警告。

3.信任制比赛巡场裁判员操作步骤

在信任制比赛中，场上出现争议需要裁判员解决，巡场裁判员应遵循对球不对人、对事不对人的处理问题的原则，以服务运动员的态度做出决定并按以下操作步骤解决问题。

（1）问：谁先申诉先问谁。

（2）听：听他们叙述事情中的共同点和不同点。

（3）看：看他们在叙述事情中的心态变化。

（4）判断：根据他们叙述的共同点和不同点，以及潜在的问题，判断他们问题的所在。

（5）决定：根据规则及处理问题的原则给出最终的决定。

第六章 判例分析

1. 判例

（1）运动员B接发球下网，将球捡起后找裁判员申诉，球破了，作为裁判你会如何判罚？

　　A. 更换该球，重赛该分　　B. 更换该球，运动员B失分

（2）运动员A发出旋转很强的外角球，运动员B从边线外将球击回，球擦到网柱上的紧网器后落入对方有效区域，A未能触到该球，作为裁判你将判谁得分？

　　A. A得分　　　　　　　B. B得分

（3）运动员球拍内加入了会影响击球特性的装置，到场地后询问主裁判是否可以使用该球拍，主裁判是否有权利允许或者禁止他使用该球拍？

　　A. 可以　　　　　　　　B. 不可以

（4）发球员将球发出的同时，球拍脱手，在球落地前球拍碰到了球网，球落到了对面发球区以外的地面，这时该怎么判罚？

　　A. 失分　　　　　　　　B. 发球失误

（5）双打比赛中，发球运动员发出的球出界，但在球落地前，接球方网前的运动员球拍触网，应当如何判罚？

　　A. 接球方失分　　　B. 发球失误　　　C. 重赛该分

（6）运动员救一个小球，击球后球落入对方有效区域，对方未能回球，但由于惯性在球落地前该击球运动员越过了球网的假定延长线，应怎么判罚？

　　A. 该击球运动员得分　　B. 该击球运动员失分

（7）运动员A放小球，运动员B将球拍抛出击到该球，并且该球过网落入有效区后运动员A未能回击该球，应判谁得分？

　　A. 运动员A得分　　　　B. 运动员B得分

（8）双打中，发球方发出的球，擦网后击中了接球方站在网前的运动员，如何判罚？

A. 发球方得分　　　　B. 发球方失分　　　C. 重发球　　　　D. 重赛球

（9）挑高球过网后，球飞向底线，球飞得很高，运动员A站在底线后2米左右准备回击该球，但球直接飞向A，球落地前，A用拍将球挡出，并呼喊"Out"，球下网，应该怎样判罚？

A. 运动员A得分　　　B. 运动员A失分

（10）一名运动员接住对手击过来的球并停止比赛，因为他看到另一片场地的球滚到对手的场地，干扰了对手的击球，裁判员应如何判罚？

A. 重赛该分　　　　　B. 接住该球的运动员失分

（11）比赛中A挑高球，擦到球场上空正好飞过的一只鸟，球刚落下对手B打高压得分，裁判员如何判罚？

A. 干扰，重赛　　　　B. 运动员B高压得分

（12）运动员A一发下网，球滚到场地中间停住，二发后对手B回球，正好打在其一发停在场地内的球上改变了方向，A无法回球，并提醒裁判员说刚才这球干扰了，主裁判怎么判罚？

A. 干扰，重赛　　　　B. A失分　　　　　C. B失分

（13）运动员A击球时帽子掉在场地上了，对手B回球，正好打在帽子上改变了方向，A无法回球，并提醒裁判员说刚才这球干扰了，主裁判怎么判罚？

A. 干扰，重赛　　　　B. A失分　　　　　C. B失分

（14）双打比赛，运动员A接发，对手球发出后还未落入发球区，A的搭档迅速跨入该发球区准备抢网，是否可以？

A. 可以　　　　　　　B. 不可以

（15）运动员A回击球的同时，司线员呼报出界，主裁判却做了好球手势，A回球出界，此时主裁判怎么判罚？

A. A失分　　　　　　B. A得分　　　　　C. 重赛

（16）运动员发出的球压在线上并直接得分，副裁判员呼报"Fault"后，主裁判立即更正，更正后该怎么判罚图（6-1）？

A. 重赛　　　　　　　B. 重发　　　　　　C. 发球得分

图6-1 副裁判员判发球失误

（17）运动员第二发球，球没抛好，直接用手接住，作为主裁判，你怎么办？

　　A. 呼报"Fault"　　　B. 呼报"Double fault"　　C. 没有任何呼报，继续比赛

（18）发出的球触到网柱后弹入对应的发球区，主裁判如何判罚？

　　A. 判发球失误　　　　B. 重发　　　　C. 重赛

（19）发球员发球同时，口袋里的球掉到地上，主裁判怎么判罚？

　　A. 不做判罚，比赛继续　B. 重赛该分，并对运动员提出警告

　　C. 发球运动员发球失误

（20）团体赛中，赛制为双-单-双，某队主教练在出场顺序表第一场双打中填了运动员A，第三场双打中也填了运动员A，前面两场结束后，比分为1∶1，此时对方主教练向主裁判提出出场顺序表的问题，作为主裁判，怎么判罚？

　　A. 要主教练更改名单　B. 判该队这场弃权，对手获胜

（21）球砸在底线上，运动员未能回球，这时司线员因为运动员的跑动未能看到落点，但副裁判员看清了这球的落点，副裁判员是否可以提示司线员这球是好球？

　　A. 可以　　　　　　　B. 不可以

第六章 判例分析

（22）运动员A击球，球过网后落在副裁判员一侧的边线处，其对手B未能回球，副裁判员对球的落点是否出界不是很确定，作为副裁判员是否可以去查看落点，再做判罚？

A. 不可以　　　　　　B. 可以

（23）运动员A在网前放小球后，球贴着网弹起，对手B冲过去击球，运动员A故意在网前挥动球拍，并叫喊影响对手击球，运动员B未能回球，作为主裁判怎么判罚（图6-2）？

A. 重赛该分　　　　B. 运动员A失分　　　C. 运动员B失分

图6-2　奋力救球

（24）运动员A追赶对手B放的一个小球，冲到主裁判座椅附近将球回过去后，由于惯性扶了下主裁判座椅才站稳，对手回球下网，作为主裁判怎么判罚？

A. 重赛该分　　　　B. 运动员A得分　　　C. 运动员B得分

（25）决胜局比分8∶8，主裁判应该怎么呼报？

A. Eight all　　　　B. Deuce　　　　C. Deuce again

（26）常规局，比分3∶3的呼报是"Three all"，4∶4时呼报"Deuce"。

A. 正确　　　　　　B. 错误

（27）第三局比赛开始，局比分1∶1，由运动员A发球，主裁判还没对局比分进行宣告，运动员A就将球发出，这时怎么处理？

A. 比赛继续　　　　B. 运动员A失分　　　C. 重发球

67

（28）副裁判员判罚了他这一侧的一个近线球为界外球，主裁判对此球的落点不是很确定，所以没有改判，这时，击球员向主裁判询问，主裁判如何回答？

　　A. 对不起，我没看清　　B. 我看到的和副裁判员的一致　C. 请裁判长解决

（29）双打比赛中，A/B为一队，A先发球，第三分，A一发下网后发现应该轮到B发球，主裁判这时也意识到轮换的错误，作为主裁判，怎么处理？

　　A. 立即更正，B发二发　　B. 立即更正，B发一发　　　C. 直接失分

（30）双打比赛，A、B两名运动员为一对，应该由A接发，但A、B站位错误，变为B接发了，B回球后，主裁判发现了他们的站位错误，这时主裁判怎么处理？

　　A. 比赛继续　　　　　B. 停止比赛，重赛该分　　C. 判A、B失分

（31）双打比赛中，发球员在右边半场发球，其搭档在发球员击球前站在发球员所在半场的发球区，对手向裁判员申诉，称其干扰到接球员对发球的判断，作为主裁判怎么判罚？

　　A. 要求发球员的搭档，站到左边半场

　　B. 告诉接球员，对手并未违反规则

（32）运动员A击球后，球压底线，对手B击球回球下网，B击球后但在球下网前，司线员做了出界的手势，主裁判确定该球压线，该怎么处理？

　　A. A得分　　　　　B. B得分　　　　　C. 重赛

（33）比赛过程中，副裁判员手势示意球出界，击球员觉得此球压线是好球，提出异议，主裁判要求副裁判员检查球印，副裁判员找不到球印，主裁判也找不到球印，此时主裁判怎么判？

　　A. 重赛　　　　　B. 请裁判长　　　C. 维持原判

（34）主裁判呼报"Out"，击球员有异议，绕过球网到对方的场地找球印，主裁判怎么处理？

　　A. 更改自己的判罚　　B. 维持原判　　C. 正式警告（黄牌）

（35）球落在运动员A半场的底线，A未能回球，并向裁判员示意球出界，主裁判走下椅子查看球印，走到半场时，A用脚擦掉球印，作为主裁判怎么判罚？

　　A. 重赛　　　　　B. 尊重A的判断，因为球在他这边他看得更清楚

C. 判对手得分,因为主裁判没判球出界

D. 判A干扰失分,并予警告

(36)运动员脚误,司线员没有呼报,主裁判可否呼报(图6-3)?

A. 可以　　　　　　　B. 不可以

图6-3　正在观察发球脚误的裁判员

(37)运动员A、B与运动员C、D进行双打,决胜局,A发第一个球,此时运动员D接球,第七分球由谁发?

A. A发球　　　　B. B发球　　　　C. C发球　　　　D. D发球

(38)中心标志的长度应该是多少?

A. 15厘米　　　　B. 10厘米　　　　C. 5厘米

(39)决胜局交换场区时,运动员A因为疲劳,坐下来休息,裁判员提醒后仍拒绝开始比赛,此时主裁判怎么处理?

A. 正式警告　　　　　　B. 判罚干扰比赛

（40）运动员受伤要治疗，主裁判通知请医生，计时应从什么时候开始？

A. 通知到医生后　　　　B. 医生进到场地后

C. 医生开始检查　　　　D. 医生开始治疗

（41）一场比赛中一名运动员可以连续接受几次医疗暂停？

A. 一次　　　　　　　　B. 两次　　　　　　　　C. 三次

（42）运动员A和B进行比赛，A挑边获胜，选择发球，B选择场地，比赛进行到局比分2：2，因下雨比赛暂停，此时A在主裁判座椅左边，B在主裁判座椅右边，比赛延期到第二天举行并换到室内场地，比赛开始前，他们应该分别站在哪边？

A. A在主裁判座椅左边，B在主裁判座椅右边

B. B在主裁判座椅左边，A在主裁判座椅右边

C. 由A重新选择　　　　D. 由B重新选择

（43）团体赛按双-单-双的顺序进行，比赛结束双方行礼后，负队教练员向主裁判申诉，对手的第一双打和第三双打运动员交换了出场顺序，主裁判报告裁判长后裁判长该怎么处理？

A. 比赛结束，不得再提出申诉　　　　B. 取消对手比赛资格

C. 重新比赛

（44）团体赛按双-单-双的顺序进行，第三双打开始后，教练员向主裁判申诉，对手的第一双打和第三双打运动员交换了出场顺序，主裁判报告裁判长后裁判长该怎么处理？

A. 重新比赛　　　　B. 取消对手比赛资格

（45）比赛开始后，运动员迟到多久，裁判员可判取消其比赛资格？

A. 5分钟　　　　　　　B. 10分钟　　　　　　　C. 15分钟

（46）双打比赛分与分之间，某队两搭档商量时间比较久影响了比赛进度，主裁判应用什么呼报来催促其尽快比赛？

A. Time　　　　　　　B. No time

（47）双打比赛中，单数局交换场地后，A、B为搭档，应该由A发球，但B站到一区端线后准备发球，这时被主裁判发现，主裁判应立即做出什么呼报？

A. Change side　　　B. Change service　　　C. Rotation change

（48）运动员用下手切削发球，由于摩擦比较强，球在球拍上滚动的轨迹比较长，主裁判呼报"Dribble"，是否符合规则（图6-4）？

A. 符合　　　　　　　B. 不符合

图6-4　下手切削发球的运动员

（49）一名运动员网前截击，贴网放了个很短的小球，由于离网太近，拍面碰球后，触到球网，但对手无论如何都接不到该球了，此时裁判员如何判罚（图6-5）？

A. 该运动员得分　　　B. 该运动员失分　　　C. 重赛

图6-5　网前截击的运动员

（50）运动员发球后，副裁判员做出发球失误的手势，对手未击球，但主裁判并未发现发球失误的情况，经主裁判询问后，副裁判员解释他看到发球错区，所以判发球失误，作为主裁判如何判罚？

A. 尊重副裁判员的判罚　　　B. 重发球　　　C. 重赛

2. 解答

（1）选B项。规则规定，比赛中，球破损时，该分仍然有效。

（2）选B项。网柱外侧附属的紧网器，应视为网柱的一部分。

（3）选B项。球拍附加其他特殊装置，比赛中该球拍是否可以使用，由裁判长决定。

（4）选A项。活球期运动员球拍触网。

（5）选A项。活球期运动员触网。

（6）选A项。如果运动员没有触及对方的场地，则不算违例。

（7）选A项。击球时球拍不能离手。

（8）选C项。符合重发球规定。

（9）选B项。击球前，还未成死球，A回球下网。

（10）选B项。是否受到干扰由主裁判决定，中断比赛的一方失分。

（11）选A项。形成了干扰的事实。

（12）选B项。符合竞赛规则中对比赛中失分情况的规定。

（13）选B项。符合竞赛规则中对比赛中失分情况的规定。

（14）选B项。违反接发球站位的规定。

（15）选C项。运动员受到裁判员干扰。依据规则中重赛球的条例。

（16）选C项。接球方无法回球的情况，裁判员虽然做出了错误的判罚，但并未形成干扰，所以发球方直接得分。

（17）选B项。发球时，球抛起而未击球属于发球失误。

（18）选B项。符合竞赛规则对重发球的规定。

（19）选A项。这种情况不属于发球失误，也不属于干扰，比赛继续。

（20）选B项。符合规则中对弃权的规定。

（21）选A项。裁判员对自己负责区域的判罚无法正确判断时，可以征求其他裁判员的意见再做判定。

第六章 判例分析

（22）选B项。不管在什么类型的场地进行比赛，均可对不确定的落点球印进行检查后再做出判罚。

（23）选B项。符合失分的规则，有明显的妨碍对手击球的情况。

（24）选C项。活球期运动员的球拍、身体或衣物触到该球场的裁判员座椅或裁判员时，判失分。

（25）选C项。决胜局6∶6报Deuce，之后的平分都呼报Deuce again。

（26）选A项。常规局各得3分或决胜局各得6分时，呼报Deuce。

（27）选C项。不符合对发球时机的规定。

（28）选B项。对于不确定的球，主裁判必须尊重副裁判员的判罚，不得轻易改判。

（29）选B项。一发失误，发现轮换有错误时，立即更正，第一次发球。

（30）选C项。同一局中不得更换接球顺序，如有违反则失一分。

（31）选B项。规则并未规定发球时发球员的搭档禁止进入发球员半区的场地。

（32）选A项。司线员的手势是在运动员B击球以后，司线员的呼报并未干扰到该名运动员击球。

（33）选C项。无法找到球印，维持原来的呼报。

（34）选C项。依照竞赛规则，此种情况可正式警告。

（35）选D项。禁止将球印擦掉，如擅自擦掉球印，属于干扰，并可按规则给予正式警告。

（36）选A项。主裁判非常确定有脚误的行为发生可以立即呼报。

（37）选C项。决胜局第三、四分的发球由接第一分发球的运动员发球，由此推算，第七分由运动员C发球。

（38）选A项。规则规定15厘米。

（39）选A项。依照规则可给予警告。

（40）选B项。医生进到场地即开表计时。

（41）选B项。医疗暂停每次5分钟，每场比赛最多两次，也可以连续。

（42）选D项。因比赛场地的变更及时间的延后，场区的选择应由原来选择场区的运动员进行选择。

（43）选A项。比赛结束，运动员相互行礼后，不得再提出申诉。

（44）选B项。根据规则规定，此种情况裁判长可直接取消队伍比赛资格。

（45）选B项。按规则规定10分钟。

（46）选B项。按规则规定NO time。

（47）选C项。对运动员与搭档之间做出交换接发球或发球的顺序做出的指令Rotation change。

（48）选B项。切削的方法发球，球拍与球的接触应视为一次击球。

（49）选B项。球在成死球前该运动员触网，应判该运动员失分。

（50）选B项。发球中线由主裁判负责判罚，副裁判员无权进行判罚，该情况符合重发球的判定。

附　录

附录 1

软式网球比赛术语

编号	术语	说明
1	预备（Ready）	开始比赛前，告诉运动员停止练习，各就位准备开始比赛的宣告
2	发球方（Service side）	比赛中发球的一边
3	接球方（Receive side）	比赛中接球的一边
4	七局比赛（Seven game match）	一场比赛采用七局制（五局、九局或三盘等也可举行）
5	比赛开始（Play ball）	比赛开始的宣告
6	重发球（Let）	发球员应重新发球。此时主裁判应宣告"Let"后并宣告"再发两次球（Two more service）或再发一次球（One more service）"
7	脚误（Foot fault）	发球者违反规则关于发球位置的限定时，该发球为失误
8	失误（Fault）	发球者违反关于发球失误的规则时，该发球失误
9	双误（Double faults）	第一次及第二次发球都失误，发球者失分
10	比赛中（In play）	开始发球到该球被判定为重发球、重赛球、失误或得失分确定的这段时间
11	界内球（In）	比赛中的球，落到球场界内或界线上
12	界外球（Out）	击出的球落在界外时，或球在落地之前直接接触到裁判员、裁判台、其他设施或设备时
13	直接球（Direct）	1.发球直接接触到接球方的身体、衣物或者球拍时，接球方应失分； 2.运动员用球拍在场地外直接触到对方击过来尚未落地的球时，该运动员失分，但运动员在场地外直接用球拍回击球有效，比赛继续进行
14	重赛球（No count）	适用于"重赛球"的竞赛规则，因某种原因重赛这一分，该分不予计分
15	暂停（Time）	适用于"暂停"的竞赛规则，因某种原因而停止比赛时
16	暂停终止（No time）	暂停时间结束，继续比赛
17	触网（Net touch）	比赛中运动员的球拍、身体、服装或者其他物品触及到球网或网柱，该运动员失分

（续表）

编号	术语	说明
18	触及（Touch）	比赛中运动员的球拍、身体、服装或其他所属物品触及到裁判员座椅或裁判员时，该运动员失分
19	过网击球（Net over）	比赛中运动员的球拍、身体、服装或运动员的其他所属物的一部分越过球网，该运动员失分；但如果是由于运动员击球后的惯性顺势过网，并没有妨碍到对方时，则不失分
20	穿网球（Through）	击出的球从网孔、球网下方或球网与网柱之间穿过时，击球方失分
21	触身球（Body touch）	比赛中的球，直接触到运动员的身体或衣物时，该运动员失分
22	擦拍（Tip）	比赛中的球，只触到球拍的拍框而未能有效还击时，该运动员失分
23	两跳（Two bounces）	比赛中，运动员回击球时球已经反弹两次，该运动员失分
24	连击（Dribble）	击球时，球触到该运动员的球拍达两次及以上时，该运动员失分，发球时则为失误
25	持球（Carry）	球在球拍上有明显的停滞现象时，该运动员失分
26	干扰（Interfere）	适用于规则"接球时失分"中3、4条，"比赛中的失分"中第5、8、9、11中部分条款，以及"接球的顺序"第一条被发现时；如果运动员擅自擦掉球印，也可视为干扰而失分
27	更正（Correction）	主裁判已经做出错误的宣告或比分宣告出现错误的情况下的宣告
28	交换场区（Change sides）	令运动员交换场区的宣告
29	交换发球（Change service）	令运动员交换发球的宣告
30	交换顺序（Rotation change）	命令运动员与其搭档交换接发球或发球顺序的宣告
31	继续比赛（Let's play）	主裁判令运动员继续进行比赛的宣告
32	弃权（Retirement）	宣判弃权，由对方获胜
33	取消资格（Disqualification）	宣判失去资格，由对方获胜
34	暂停时间到，比赛结束（Time's up and game set）	违反竞赛规则"弃权"中第3、4条时的宣告，由对方获胜

(续表)

编号	术语	说明
35	裁判长宣告停止比赛，比赛结束（Referee stop and game set）	违反竞赛规则"弃权"第5条及"取消资格"中的条款时的宣告，对方获胜
36	1∶0/0∶1（One zero/Zero one）	发球方（接球方）得1分，而接球方（发球方）未得分时
37	2∶0/0∶2（Two zero/Zero two）	发球方（接球方）得2分，而接球方（发球方）未得分时
38	3∶0/0∶3（Three zero/Zero three）	发球方（接球方）得3分，而接球方（发球方）未得分时
39	2∶1/1∶2（Two one/One two）	发球方（接球方）得2分，而接球方（发球方）得1分时
40	3∶1/1∶3（Three one/One three）	发球方（接球方）得3分，而接球方（发球方）得1分时
41	3∶2/2∶3（Three two/Two three）	发球方（接球方）得3分，而接球方（发球方）得2分时
42	1∶1（One all）	双方各得1分时
43	2∶2（Two all）	双方各得2分时
44	3∶3（Three all）	双方各得3分时
45	3∶4/4∶3（Three four/Four three）	发球方（接球方）得3分，而接球方（发球方）得4分时
46	3∶5/5∶3（Three five/Five three）	发球方（接球方）得3分，而接球方（发球方）得5分时
47	4∶0/0∶4）（Four zero/Zero four）	发球方（接球方）得4分，而接球方（发球方）未得分时
48	4∶1/1∶4（Four one/One four）	发球方（接球方）得4分，而接球方（发球方）得1分时
49	4∶2/2∶4（Four two/Two four）	发球方（接球方）得4分，而接球方（发球方）得2分时
50	5∶0/0∶5（Five zero/Zero five）	发球方（接球方）得5分，而接球方（发球方）未得分时
51	5∶1/1∶5（Five one/One five）	发球方（接球方）得5分，而接球方（发球方）得1分时

（续表）

编号	术语	说明
52	5：2/2：5（Five two/Two five）	发球方（接球方）得5分，而接球方（发球方）得2分时
53	5：4/4：5（Five four/Four five）	发球方（接球方）得5分，而接球方（发球方）得4分时
54	4：4（Four all）	双方各得4分时
55	5：5（Five all）	双方各得5分时
56	6：0/0：6（Six zero/Zero six）	发球方（接球方）得6分，而接球方（发球方）未得分时
57	6：1/1：6（Six one/One six）	发球方（接球方）得6分，而接球方（发球方）得1分时
58	6：2/2：6（Six two/Two six）	发球方（接球方）得6分，而接球方（发球方）得2分时
59	6：1/1：6（Six three/Three six）	发球方（接球方）得6分，而接球方（发球方）得3分时
60	6：4/4：6（Six four/Four six）	发球方（接球方）得6分，而接球方（发球方）得4分时
61	6：5/5：6（Six five/Five six）	发球方（接球方）得6分，而接球方（发球方）得5分时
62	平分（Deuce）	双方各得3分或决胜局中双方各得6分
63	发球方（接发球方）领先 Advantage server（receiver）	平分后发球方（接发球方）得1分
64	再平分（Deuce again）	平分后先得1分，得1分方未能继续赢得下1分，使双方再变成平分时
65	局的比赛结束（Game）	每局比赛结束时的宣告
66	局的比数（Game count）	比赛双方所得局数，于下一局比赛开始前宣告，发球方的局数在前。双方运动员各得三局或四局时，应宣告"三平"或"四平"，而不能宣告"平分"或"再平分"
67	决胜局（Final game）	七局制比赛时各得三局或九局制比赛各得四局，为表示将进入最后一局的比赛。在宣告三平（四平）后，加上"决胜局"的宣告
68	比赛结束（Game set）	该场比赛全部结束后的宣告

附录2

软式网球比赛记分表
Soft Tennis score sheet

Score Sheet for Doubles/Singles
双打/单打记分表

Game 比赛：	Men 男 Women 女	Court No. 场地：	Chair Umpire 主裁判：	Vice Umpire 副裁判员：
Round 场次(轮次)：		Time Started 开始时间： Time Finished 结束时间：	Linesman(1) 司线员(1)：	Linesman(2) 司线员(2)：

Team No. 队号	Team Name 队名		Score 得分	Team No. 队号	Team Name 队名	
Player 队员	A B		-	Player 队员	A B	
SR			-(1)-	SR		
SR			-(2)-	SR		
SR			-(3)-	SR		
SR			-(4)-	SR		
SR			-(5)-	SR		
SR			-(6)-	SR		
SR			-(7)-	SR		
SR			-(8)-	SR		
SR			-(F)-	SR		

Warning 警告	Y	Y	R	Time A: 5 . 5 B: 5 . 5	Time A: 5 . 5 B: 5 . 5	Warning 警告	Y	Y	R
Remarks 记录						Remarks 记录			

Winner's Signature 获胜者（签名）：	Chair Umpire 主裁判：	Referee 裁判长：	Recorded 竞赛组（记录组）：

附录 3

竞赛器材清单

序号	器材名称	数量	备注
1	软式网球		
2	主裁判座椅		
3	司线员座椅		
4	运动员休息椅		
5	饮水机		
6	遮阳伞		
7	量网尺		
8	记分牌		
9	秒表		
10	裁判包		
11	无线麦克风		
12	推水器		
13	拖把		
14	垃圾桶		
15	观众席		
16	办公桌椅		
17	电脑		
18	打印机、复印机		
19	传真机		
20	穿线机		

注：其他物品需求根据实际情况进行考虑。

附录4

裁判长、副裁判长及仲裁具体工作任务

一、裁判长

（一）赛前工作

1. 熟悉竞赛规程，全面了解场地、器材、设备情况，制订裁判工作计划。
2. 深入了解裁判员的思想品质、业务素质和身体健康状况，合理分工。
3. 了解编排工作情况，重点是审查比赛秩序和每个单元安排情况，精确估算时间，做到准时开始，按时结束。
4. 组织全体裁判员学习竞赛规程和竞赛规则，研究裁判法，督促裁判组制订工作细则。
5. 组织各裁判组仔细检查场地、器材和设备，发现问题及时解决。
6. 组织裁判进行现场实习，使裁判员明确岗位职责、活动范围、进出场路线，熟练掌握裁判法。
7. 在技术会议上宣布竞赛的有关规定。

（二）赛中工作

1. 每单元比赛开始前，按规定时间检查各裁判组到场情况，督促各裁判组准时组织比赛。
2. 掌握各项比赛进程。在比赛中如遇特殊情况（如狂风暴雨），比赛不能继续进行时，应与技术代表和竞委会负责人共同研究停赛或开赛的时间。
3. 裁判长席位一般设在可全面观察比赛情况的位置。对有可能发生问题的项目和场地，应亲临现场或多加注意，以便发现问题能及时处理。
4. 根据规则解决比赛中各种疑难问题。遇运动员与裁判员的意见不一致时，应认真了解情况，并根据规则规定妥善解决。
5. 每天比赛结束后，应根据需要召开裁判工作会议，及时了解当天的比赛情况及存在问题，提出解决办法和应对措施。如遇特殊情况，可随时召开相关人员会议，研究和解决问题。

（三）赛后工作

1. 比赛结束后，宣布比赛成绩。
2. 领导全体裁判员做好总结工作。
3. 做好赛后工作，如有关资料归档等。

二、副裁判长

1. 协助裁判长组织、领导裁判工作，保证裁判工作的顺利进行。
2. 裁判长在缺席时，指定一名副裁判长代理其职务，或委托其处理有关事宜。
3. 根据裁判长建议，分工领导赛前和赛后工作，但不能取代裁判长的工作。
4. 检查各种通讯设备情况，及时了解所分管的各裁判组的情况，督促、检查他们的工作。
5. 比赛中亲临现场，发现问题及时与主裁判商讨解决，解决不了时要及时报告裁判长研究解决。
6. 组织协调和维护比赛秩序，检查各项比赛的安全措施。
7. 负责裁判组的生活安排。

三、仲裁委员会

1. 处理各项抗议，同时对发生于比赛中提交仲裁委员会的其他事宜做出裁决。仲裁委员会的裁决为最终裁决。
2. 凡对规则未涉及的问题做出裁决，事后应由仲裁委员会主任向有关软式网球协会报告。

附录 5

国际软式网球联合会规则（英文版）

Rules of Soft Tennis
Rules for Competitions
DOUBLES

Chapter 1 General Rules

(Purpose)

● 1

The provisions hereunder shall aim to specify the matters to be required to conduct soft tennis competitions (doubles).

Chapter 2 Court for Soft Tennis

(Soft Tennis Court)

● 2

A soft tennis court shall consist of Court, Outcourt, Net and Net Post and Umpire's Chair.

(Court and Outcourt)

● 3

A court and outcourt shall be the same flat space which shall be maintained so as not to cause any hindrance to the play. For the out-door court, however, a slight slope for water drainage shall be allowed to be constructed to the extent that no hindrance to the play shall be caused.

(Surface of Court and Outcourt)

● 4

The surface of a court and outcourt shall be clay, sanded artificial grass, all-weather chemical or other appropriate materials for the outdoor court, and for the indoor court, the surface shall be wooden, sanded artificial grass, hard rubber, chemical or other appropriate materials.

(Court)

● 5

The court for doubles shall be a rectangular space, which shall be surrounded by lines (the lines are part of the court), of 23.77m in length and 10.97m in width, and it shall be divided into two equal portions by the net, which is supported by the net posts, in the middle of the court.

(Divisions of Court and Lines)

● 6

The names of the divisions of a court and the names and lengths of the lines on the court are as shown hereunder.

Names of Lines Symbol Length

Sideline AC, BD 23.77m

Base Line AB, CD 10.97m

Service Sideline EG, FH 12.80m

Service Line EF, GH 8.23m

Service Center Line MN 12.80m

Center Mark R, S 0.15m(from the inner edge of the base line)

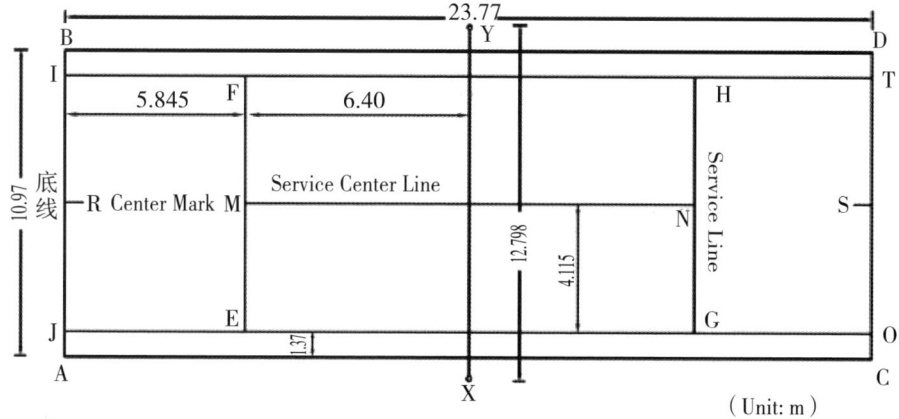

(Unit: m)

(Color, Width and Length of Line)

● 7

The lines shall, in principle, be white in color and not less than 5cm and not more than 6cm in width. The width of base lines, however, shall be more than 5cm and not more than 10cm.

(Out court)

● 8

(1) The out court shall be a space surrounding the court and the space shall spread, in principle, more than 8m from the respective base lines and more than 6m from the respective sidelines.

(2) In the case where two or more courts adjoin each other, the distance between the sidelines of the adjoining courts shall not be less than 5m in principle.

(Net Post)

● 9

The net post shall be not less than 7.5cm and not more than 15cm in diameter.

(Location of Net Post)

● 10

(1) The net posts shall be set up outside and in the middle of the sidelines on both sides of a court and fixed vertically at the equal distance from the side lines.

(2) The distance between the two posts shall be 12.80m (measured at the outside of the posts) and the height of the posts shall be 1.07m from the ground. In the case where the facility conditions do not permit such a height of the net post as above, it shall be allowed to be less than 1.07m but not less than 1.06m.

(Umpire's Chair)

● 11

The umpire's chair shall be 1.5m in height in principle and be placed in an out court, 60cm apart (at the nearest part of the chair) from a net post.

Chapter 3 Equipment

(Net)

● 12

The specifications of the net shall be as undermentioned.

(1) Color : Black.

(2) Height : 1.07m. In the case where the facility conditions do not permit this height, the height shall be allowed to be less than 1.07m, but not less than 1.06m. (The net shall be put up tightly between the posts, horizontally on a level at the height of 1.06m to 1.07m measured at the sidelines.)

(3) Length : 12.65m.

(4) Meshes : Not more than 3.5cm in square.

(5) Metal Cord : 15m in length and 4.5mm in diameter, as standard specifications.

(6) The top of a net and the metal cord shall be covered with a white cloth band of 5cm to 6cm in width.

(7) Both ends of a net shall be kept touching to the net posts and the lowest part of the net to the ground.

(Ball)

● 13

The ball shall be rubber-made, air-filled, and its color shall be white in principle. The specifications of the ball shall be as undermentioned.

(1) The bounce of a ball shall be adjusted so that the highest point that the ball reaches after it bounced on the court comes to not less than 70cm and not more than 80cm (measured at the bottom of the ball) from the ground when dropped without putting any intentional force from a height of 1.5m from the ground upon the court where the match is to be played.

(2) Weight : not less than 30g and not more than 31g.

(3) Diameter : 6.6cm with a allowance of plus or minus 0.1cm.

(Racket)

● 14

(1) The racket shall be the one which is designed to achieve the same effect at its both faces with its frame strung with strings and its strung face shall be flat. The condition of strings after strung shall be practicably even.

(2) The frame of a racket shall be allowed to be of any material and weight, and in any size and shape.

(3) The strings shall be fixed to the frame of a racket and shall be crossed each other.

(4) The strings shall not be of specifications which may provide a ball with excessive variations in flying.

Chapter 4   Competitions
(Player's Conduct)

● 15

Players shall mutually respect good manners and observe the codes of conduct as under mentioned.

(1) Players shall not excessively yell out or make much noises which may cause discomfort for their opponent.

(2) Players shall play continuously from the start to the finish of a match, and the behaviors as under mentioned are prohibited. An allowance of one (1) minute shall be allowed before they get ready to start a next point or game after the completion of the previous point or game, when they change sides or before starting the final game or when they change sides after having finished 10 points in a short match as provided in Article 17.2 of this Rules ("Let's Play").

a. A server intentionally delays delivering a serve, even when the receiver of the serve is ready to receive, and likewise, the receiver of a serve does not get ready to receive even when the server is about to deliver the serve.

b. A player intentionally acts to make the match drag on.

c. A pair of players in doubles make lengthy arrangements with each other or take a rest between points or games, thus obstruct the progress of the match.

d. A player does not get ready to start the next game within the allowed time after the previous game was completed.

e. A player takes a rest while changing sides in the final game.

f. A player repairs its racket during a match.

(3) Players shall follow the instructions given by the umpire in proceeding the match.

(Match)

● 16

(1) Players shall always abide by this Rules and keep to a fair play throughout a match.

(2) A doubles match is organized by 2 pairs and each pair consists of 2 players. Each player shall play with one racket throughout a match.

(3) A ball shall be struck alternately by one or the other player of the opposing pairs.

(The Number of Games in a Match)

● 17

(1) A match shall be played by a 7 or 9 games system in principle.

(2) Short matches like a 15-point match, a 3-game match or a 5-game match can be played. Long matches like a 3-set match or a 5-set match can also be played, wherein one set consists of 15 points by a 3, 5, 7 or 9 games.

(Win or Loss of a Game)

● 18

(1) A pair who has first won four points in a game shall win the game. When both pairs won three points in a game, the score shall be called deuce, and the procedures as under mentioned shall be applied.

a. The pair who has won one point after deuce gets advantage, and when the same pair has won the next point in succession, the game shall be scored for the pair.

b. When, after the advantage for one pair, the other pair has won the following point, the score shall be called deuce again. The same procedures shall be followed as far as the same proceeding of a game as above continues.

(2) When both pairs won three games in a 7-game match, the following 7th game shall be called the final game, and the procedures as undermentioned shall be applied. The same procedures shall be applied for 3-, 5- or 9-game matches, i.e. when both pairs won 1 game in a 3-game match, 2 games in a 5-game match or 4 games in a 9-game match.

a. Notwithstanding the provisions in Article 18.1 above, the pair who has won 7 points in the final game shall win the game and the match.

b. When both pairs won six points in the final game, the score shall be called deuce, and the provisions in Article "a" above shall be applied.

(3) For a 15-point match, the final game shall be played according to Article of this Rules, and the pair who has first won 15 points shall win the game and the match. In the case where both pairs won 14 points, the score shall be called deuce, and Article 18 (1) above shall be applied.

(Win or Loss of a Match)

- 19

(1) In the case of a match of 3 or more odd games, the pair who has first won the majority of the games shall win the match.

(2) In the case of a match of 3 or more odd sets, the pair who has first won the majority games of each set shall win the set, and who has first won the majority of the sets shall win the match.

(Serve)

- 20

(1) The play of serve shall start at the moment when a player who is going to deliver the serve has tossed (The word "toss" means for a server to leave a ball from its hand to deliver a serve. Hereinafter this word shall be used in the same meaning.) up into the air by hand and shall complete at the moment when the player has struck the ball with its racket before it drops on either of the court or outcourt. In the case where a server has failed to hit at ball in trying to deliver a serve, the serve shall be regarded as completed at the moment when the ball may have touched the racket of the server in serving. The judgment of this shall be made by the chair umpire.

(2) A player who is limited to use only one arm/hand for the play shall be allowed to

utilize its racket for tossing a ball.

(Time of Serving)

● 21

A server shall deliver a serve following the chair umpire's call on scores, after confirming the receiver's readiness.

(Servers & Receivers)

● 22

Each pair shall stand face to face with the net between them and the pair who delivers the serve shall be called Servers and the other pair who shall receive the serve shall be called Receivers.

(Position for Serving)

● 23

A server shall deliver a serve from behind the base line and between the imaginary extensions of the center mark and the sideline.

(Player to Serve)

● 24

(1) A serve shall be delivered by one of the servers, who shall deliver the serve to the diagonally opposite service court, starting from the right side of the center mark facing the net, and then from the left.

(2) Each player of the servers whose turn it is to serve shall alternately serve for two consecutive points, and the initial order of service shall not be changed in the same one game.

(Fault in the Serve)

● 25

(1) The cases where the serve is defined as a fault are as undermentioned.

a. A ball served has failed to fall directly into a proper service court, except for the cases of a let as provided in Article 26 of this Rules.

b. A server did not struck a ball after having tossed it in the air for delivering a serve.

c. Two balls have been tossed at the same time in delivering a serve, or one of the two balls for the serve has dropped from the server's hand while the other ball was tossed up but not yet struck for the serve.

d. A ball has come into contact with the server's racket more than once in delivering a serve.

e. A ball served has come under either of the provisions as undermentioned after the ball touched the net or the net post and before it hits the court, outcourt, fences, etc.

> i. The ball has touched the server's racket (including a racket which had left from the server's hand), body or attire (including a cap or a hat, a face towel, glasses, etc. which the server was wearing).(Hereinafter the word "attire" shall mean the same.)
>
> ii. The server's racket (including a racket which had left from the server's hand), body or attire has passed over or touched the net or the net post, before the ball hits the court, outcourt umpire's chair, fences, etc.

f. A server has touched the base-line, sideline or center mark, or gone into the inside of the court while delivering a serve (Foot Fault). However, the case where the server has moved over the base line into the court but was still in space while delivering the serve shall not come under this clause.

(2) The server, if the first serve turned a fault, shall be allowed to deliver the second serve.

(Let in the Serve)

● 26

(1) The cases where the serve shall be defined as a let shall be as undermentioned.

a. A breach of Article 21 in this Rules has occurred, as judged by the chair umpire.

b. A ball served has come under the provisions as undermentioned after the ball touched the net or the net post.

> i. The ball has fallen into a proper service court.
>
> ii. The ball has touched the receiver's racket (including a racket which had left from the receiver's hand), body or attire before the ball hits the court, outcourt, umpire's chair and fences, etc.

iii. The receiver's racket (including a racket which had left from the receiver's hand), body or attire has passed over or touched the net or the net post.

c. The receiver of a ball served has come under the provisions as undermentioned, as judged by the chair umpire, before the receive is completed.

i. The receiver's play has been interrupted by an umpire's erroneous judgment.

ii. The receiver's play has been interrupted by unforeseen incidents or by a ball for a match at some other court or its own ball which had been picked up and thrown in by people with no direct relations with the ongoing match or acts of such people.

iii. Incidents which cause to lose a point have occurred on both pairs at the same time.

d. Other cases which the chair umpire has acknowledged as a let in the serve.

(2) When a serve has turned a let, that serve shall be tried again.

(Loss of Point in the Serve)

● 27

In the case where both the first and second serves have turned faults consecutively, the servers shall lose the point as double faults.

(Receiving the Serve)

● 28

In receiving a serve, the receiver shall return the ball legally served after its first bounce on a proper service court but before the second bounce.

(Order of Receiving the Serve)

● 29

The order of receiving the serve among the receivers shall be as undermentioned.

(1) Each of the receivers shall receive a serve at either of the right or left service court, and the order of the receiving thus initiated shall not be changed during a game.

(2) The receive shall start with the right service court and the receivers shall receive a serve alternately at the right and the left.

(Loss of Point in the Receive)

● 30

The cases where the receivers of a serve lose a point are as undermentioned.

(1) The receiver has failed to legally return the ball served.

(2) The ball served has directly touched the receiver's racket, body or attire ("Direct").

(3) The ball legally served has directly touched the racket, body or attire of the partner of the receiver before its second bounce on the ground ("Interfere").

(4) The partner of the receiver has touched the receiver's service court before the receiver completes the receive ("Interfere").

(5) A breach of Article 29 (1) in this Rules has been found ("Interfere"). This shall be applied only to the point where the breach was found.

(Choice of Serve/Receive or Side)

● 31

Serve/receive or side shall be chosen by competing pairs before the beginning of a match.

(Change of Serve/Receive and Side)

● 32

(1) Servers and receivers shall alternate serving at the completion of each game, except for the final game, and they shall change sides at every time the odd games completed.

(2) In the final game, the pairs shall alternate serving for every two points and they shall change sides after the first two points and then after every four points after that. The serve and receive in the final game shall be played as undermentioned.

a. Each player of both pairs shall serve in rotation for two consecutive points.

b. The player who serves for the first two points shall be either of the pair who has the right to be servers in accordance with the rules.

c. Either one of the players who received the first serve in the final game shall serve for the third and fourth points, and either one of the players who served for the first two points in the final game shall receive the serve for the third point.

d. The other one of the players who served for the first two points in the final game shall serve for the fifth and sixth points.

e. The other one of the players who served for the third and fourth points in the final game shall serve for the seventh and eighth points.

f. Thereafter, the orders of serve and receive shall revert to the order as provided in Items b to e above of this Article.

g. The order of serve and receive in the pair shall not be changed during a game.

(Error in Order of Serve/Receive and Side)

- 33

(1) When an error in changes of servers or sides, as under mentioned, have been found, the correction of the error shall be made as at that point if it was before the point started. If an error was found after a point had started, the point in play shall be continued without suspension and the correction of the error shall be made as at the next point. Points already played before the finding of the error shall be effective.

a. An error has occurred in changes of servers ("Change service") and sides ("Change sides").

b. An error has occurred in the order of serve between the partners ("Rotation Change").

c. An error has occurred in the order of selecting a service court ("Rotation Change").

(2) In the case where such errors have been found after a fault in the first serve, the errors shall be corrected at that instant, and the match shall be resumed with the first serve.

(Judgment of In or Out)

- 34

(1) The judgment of in or out of a ball shall be made at the landing spot of the ball.

(2) The ball which has touched the court lines when it landed on the court shall be defined as in.

(Loss of Point In Play)

● 35

The cases of loss of points in play shall be as undermentioned. However, the cases where a serve is a let or the first serve is a fault shall not come under this clause.

(1) The ball which was hit by a player has failed to directly fly over the net (no judgment call), and a ball has gone through a break of the net or a space between the net and the net post or under the net ("Through") shall come under this clause. However, the cases as undermentioned shall be excluded.

a. A ball touched the net or the net post, but has flied properly over into the opposite court.

b. A ball flied outside of the net post or touched the outside of the net post, but has landed properly on the opposite court.

(2) The ball returned has landed on an outcourt or directly touched the umpire, the umpire's chair or other fixtures and facilities for the ongoing match ("Out").

(3) A player has failed to hit the ball for a return before the ball bounces on the ground for the second time ("Two Bounces"). The case where the ball hit for a return has touched, before bouncing for the second time, the umpire, the umpire's chair or other fixtures and facilities shall also come under this clause. However, the case where the ball from the opponent landed properly on the court but rebounded to the net or the net post and the player has returned, before the ball landed on the court again, the ball properly to the opponent shall be regarded as a good return.

(4) A ball has touched the body or attire of a player ("Body Touch").

(5) Such cases as under mentioned have occurred to the racket, body or attire of a player. However, the cases where the racket has crossed over the net or touched the opponent's outcourt from force of hitting a ball but that incident was not recognized as an apparent interference with the opponent's play ("Interfere") shall not come under this clause.

a. A player's racket has crossed over the net, the imaginary extensions of the net line or the net post in a failed swing of the racket in trying to hit a ball ("Net Over").

b. The racket, body or attire of a player has touched the net or the net post ("Net Touch"). The case where a ball hit the net or the wind moved the net, as the net touched the racket, body or attire of a player shall be included.

c. The racket, body or attire of a player has touched the umpire's chair or the umpire for the ongoing match ("Touch").

d. The racket, body or attire of a player has touched the opponent's court or the racket, body or attire of the opponent player ("Interfere").

(6) A ball has touched a racket more than once in striking the ball ("Dribble") or the ball has rested on a racket face ("Carry").

(7) A ball touched only the frame of a racket in trying to hit the ball, thus the player has failed to return the ball ("Tip").

(8) A player has returned a ball by the racket which had left from its hand ("Interfere").

(9) A ball in play has hit another ball on the court, including a ball which is used for the ongoing match and had been on one side of the court when the point started but moved in by the force of wind or some other reasons and rested on the other side of the court. However, in the case where such a movement of the ball was judged by the chair umpire as an intentional act against the opponent, this constitutes an interference. Also, the case where the ball hit players' things like a hat or cap or face towel, etc. which was lying on the court, thus the player has failed to make a good return of the ball shall come under this clause.

(10) The racket, cap or hat, face towel, etc. of a player left from the player and has directly touched the net or the net post ("Net Touch"). The case where a racket once dropped from the player on the ground and then has touched the net or the net post shall be included.

(11) When a player pushed away, by its hand, foot or racket, things like a hat or a cap or face towel, etc., excluding a ball, which was lying on the court or outcourt, they have directly touched the net or net post ("Net Touch"), or the umpire or the umpire's chair for the ongoing match ("Touch").

(12) The racket, cap or hat, face towel, etc. of a player has touched the racket or attire of the opponent player or gone over into the opponent court ("Interfere").

(13) Incidents which are an apparent interference with the opponent's play have occurred (called "Interfere").

(No Count)

● 36

A play shall be suspended with a "No Count" call on the ball in play in the cases as undermentioned and the play for the point shall be resumed by starting with the first serve. The cases of a let in the serve shall not come under this clause.

(1) A play has been interrupted by an umpire's erroneous judgment.

(2) A play has been interrupted by unforeseen incidents, a ball for some other match, a ball for the ongoing match which had left away but was picked up and thrown in by people with no direct relations with the ongoing match or the acts of such people.

The application of this clause shall be limited to those acknowledged by the chair umpire.

(3) Incidents where the both pairs lose the point at the same time have occurred.

(4) Other cases which the chair umpire has acknowledged as those for no count.

(Time)

● 37

Time shall be allowed for players during a match in the cases as undermentioned.

(1) A player has turned disable to continue the play by physical problems and the chair umpire has acknowledged the situation.

In this case, the time allowable for a player shall be not more than 5 minutes per one occasion and a maximum of two occasions allowed for one player in the same one match.

(2) Other cases which the chair umpire has acknowledged as necessary.

(Prohibitions)

● 38

(1) A player shall be prohibited from receiving any advice and physical treatment from any people other than their partner during a match, except for the cases approved by the chair umpire as necessary after discussing it with the referee.

(2) Any people other than the players for the match, the umpires and those who are allowed for the specific reasons shall be prohibited from entering the soft tennis court during the match.

(Withdraw)

● 39

A pair who comes under the items as undermentioned shall be treated as the one withdrawn from the match, and their opponent shall be declared the winner of the match. Points & games so far won by such a loser shall be effective.

(1) An entry for the competition had been made but the pair did not actually participated.

(2) An application made by a pair for withdrawal from the competition for some special reasons has been accepted by the referee (or responsible officials of the competitions).

(3) Time was allowed for a pair for physical problems of either player of the pair, but the player has not recovered within the allowed time limits.

(4) Either player of the pair applied for withdrawal from the match for its physical problems and the chair umpire has accepted it.

(5) A pair has turned unable to play a match under the conditions as described in Article 11 of the Rules for Operations of Competitions.

(Prohibition of Protest and Other Related Acts)

● 40

(1) Players shall be prohibited from protesting against the umpire's proceeding of his judgments in a match or discontinuing a play on the ground that such judgments are objectionable.

(2) The provision as above, however, shall not prevent the players from inquiring of the umpire about his judgments and others. However, once the explanations have been delivered, then the provision of the proceeding Article 40 (1) shall be applied.

(Warning)

● 41

In the cases where apparent violations of Articles 38 and 40 have been recognized, the chair umpire shall give a warning to such pair ("Yellow Card").

(Disqualification)

● 42

(1) When the referee has found any violations of the conditions for participation provided in the guide to the championships, the referee shall declare the disqualification of such pair after consulting it with the responsible officials of the competitions.

(2) In the cases which come under the clauses as undermentioned, the chair umpire shall disqualify such pair and declare the winning of their opponents.

a. A pair who was called to a court for a match has not appeared.

b. The number of warnings issued has come to 3 in total to the same one pair during the same one match ("Red Card").

(Appeal)

● 43

(1) A pair shall be allowed to appeal to the referee if a misinterpretation or misapplication of the Rules for Competitions have been recognized in the judgments of the umpire.

(2) A pair shall not be allowed to appeal for the second time against the ruling made by the referee.

(3) A pair shall not be allowed to make any appeals after the greetings for the completion of the match have been exchanged.

(Suspension and Resumption of a Match)

● 44

(1) In the case where a match was suspended or postponed because of the weather condition or others, the match shall be resumed, in principle, as from the next point to those so far completed.

(2) In the case where the match is resumed at a tennis court than the current one or on a later day, the side of the court shall be selected by the pair who had the right to select it in the current match. However, in the case where the match is resumed at a later time on the same day and the same court as for the current match, the same sides as at the time

of the suspension of the match shall be maintained.

(Treatment of Other Questionable Issues on Rules)

● 45

In the cases where issues which are not specified in this Rules have occurred in a match, the chair umpire shall rule them after consulting with the referee.

SINGLES

(Purpose)

● 1

The provisions hereunder shall aim to specify the matters required to conduct soft tennis competitions (singles). The rules for doubles shall be applied for the matters not specified in the rules for singles.

(Court)

● 2

A court for singles shall be a rectangular space, which is surrounded by the service sidelines with their extensions to the base lines and the base lines, of 23.77m in length and 8.23m in width.

(Divisions of Court and Lines)

● 3

The names of the divisions of the court and the names and lengths of the lines are as shown hereunder. Names of Lines Symbol Length

Sideline AC, BD 23.77m
Base Line AB, CD 8.23m
Service Sideline EG, FH 12.80m
Service Line EF, GH 8.23m
Service Center Line MN 12.80m
Center Mark R, S 0.15m (from the inner edge of the base line)

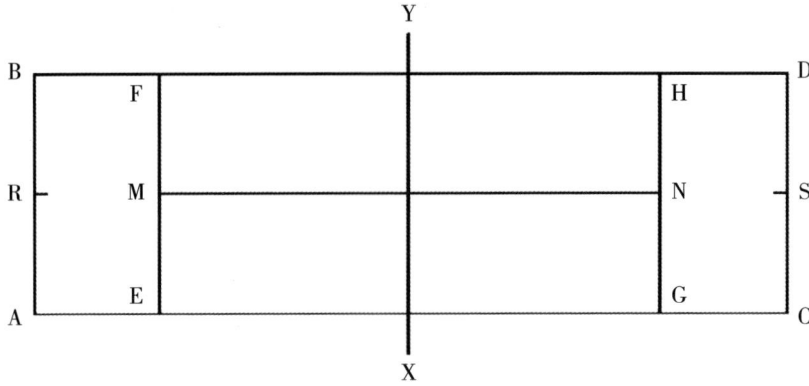

(Serve and Receive)

● 4

(1) Except for the final game, the opposing players shall deliver the serve alternately for each of the games in a match, starting to deliver the serve in each game to the right, diagonally opposite service court and then to the left, and the other player shall receive the ball served.

(2) In the final game, each of the players shall deliver the serve alternately for two consecutive points, starting with the player who has the right to be a server in accordance with the rules, and the other player shall receive the ball served.

(Match)

● 5

The number of games in a match shall be 7 in principle.

Rules for Umpiring

Chapter 1   General Rules

(Purpose)

● 1

The provisions hereunder shall be intended to specify the matters concerning umpiring for soft tennis competitions.

Chapter 2　Jury

(Jury)

● 2

(1) The jury for competitions shall consist of referees and umpires.

(2) The referees shall be more than 1 and less than 5 in number, and one of the referees shall be appointed as chief referee who shall supervise the other referees and umpires.

(3) The umpires shall be 4 in number in principle for one court for competitions. However, the total number of commissioned umpires can be reduced at a discretion of the host/managing organization for competitions in the case where the guide to the competitions provides that the participating players shall conduct umpiring for competitions.

(4) The host/managing organization for competitions may place a court supervisor at respective courts as required.

(Referee)

● 3

The referee shall give directions and advice to umpires. Also, in the case where an appeal has been made to the referee about an umpire's judgment on the ground that the judgment involves a misunderstanding or misapplication of the Rules of Soft Tennis for Competitions (Hereinafter called the "Rules for Competitions" and the Rules for Umpiring for Competitions (Hereinafter called the "Rules for Umpiring", the referee shall get a good grasp of the content of the appeal and rule the case.

(Court Supervisor)

● 4

The court supervisor shall promote the proceeding of competitions at the court in charge, and give directions and advice to umpires as required.

(Umpire)

● 5

1 chair umpire and 1 vice umpire, in principle, shall be placed for a match. However, the vice umpire may be dispensed with if appropriate. Also, 2 linesmen may additionally be placed, if required.

(Duties of Umpire)

● 6

(1) An umpire shall promote the smooth proceeding of the play and make fair and quick judgments according to the Rules for Competitions.

(2) The chair umpire shall perform its duties of proceeding with a match on the umpire's chair and make judgments on the designated areas of judgment. Regarding the judgments on the areas which the other umpires are responsible for, the chair umpire shall confirm and respect their signs and/or calls on their judgments, call its ruling clearly and enter the result in a score sheet.

(3) The vice umpire and linesmen, who place themselves at the designated positions as provided in Article 9 (2),(3) of this Rules, shall make judgments on their responsible judgment areas, and also assist the chair umpire.

(4) The vice umpire and linesmen shall notify their judgments to the chair umpire by signs when the judgments are related only to lines, and for the judgments on the other responsible judgment areas, the notification shall be made by calls together with signs.

Chapter 3　Umpiring
(Required Attitude of Umpire)

● 7

The umpire shall be well acquainted itself to the matters as undermentioned to conduct a fair and smooth proceeding of a match.

(1) The umpire shall be well versed in both the Rules for Competitions and the Rules for Umpiring, and conduct appropriate applications of them.

(2) The umpire's attire shall be those that are normally worn for soft tennis

competitions, except the case where the host/managing organization for competitions has designated the attire.

(3) While umpiring, an umpire shall observe the items as undermentioned.

a. An umpire shall prepare for its duties at a court in charge well in advance of players' appearance. If necessary, the umpire shall urge the players to appear on the court in time.

b. An umpire shall make an effort to maintain an appropriate behavior.

c. An umpire shall make an effort to conduct a smooth and fair proceeding of a match.

d. An umpire shall make an effort to make a fair and timely judgment.

e. An umpire shall make a loud and clear call on its judgment according to Article 10 of this Rules.

f. An umpire shall give a clear sign of its judgment according to Article 11 of this Rules.

g. An umpire shall keep a good coordination among its colleague umpires for the match.

h. Umpires shall not violate the authorities of their colleague umpires on their respective responsible judgment areas.

(Division of Judgment Area)

● 8

The division of the responsible judgment lines/items for the respective umpires is as under mentioned. (see the attached chart of the judgment areas):

(1) The division of the responsible judgment lines: Chair umpire AC, EG, MN, XY B Y D Vice umpire BD, FH, EF, GH, XY Linesman AB, CD.

(2) The division of other responsible judgment items.

Chair umpire: two bounces, dribble, carry, direct, interfere, body touch, touch, tip, net over, net touch, through, let, no count, foot fault.

Vice umpire: two bounces, dribble, carry, direct, interfere, body touch, touch, tip, net over, net touch, through, let, no count, foot fault.

Linesman: foot fault, direct, body touch, tip.

(3) In the case where the vice umpire and linesmen are dispensed with, their

judgment areas/lines shall be covered by the chair umpire.

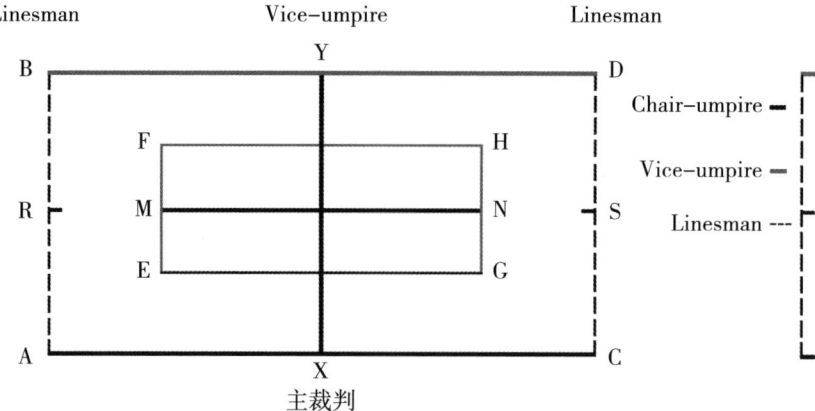

(Position of Umpire)

● 9

The positions of umpires during a match shall be as undermentioned:

(1) The chair umpire shall be seated on the umpire's chair.

(2) The viceumpire shall place itself out of the sideline on the opposite side to the the chair umpire, and 60cm apart outward from the net post. When judging a serve, the vice umpire shall move to the imaginary extension of the service line, outside of the sideline on the receiver's court. After judging a serve, the vice umpire shall return to the initial position immediately and keep watching rallies.

(3) The linesman shall be seated on a chair which is placed not less than 5m out of the sideline on the opposite side to the chair umpire's seat on the imaginary extension of the base line.

(Call)

● 10

(1) How to make calls for judgment and score-counting shall be provided on the attached sheets, glossary of Umpire's Terms and Score Counting.

(2) Calls for point and game counting shall be made by the chair umpire, starting

from those for the servers' side.

(3) When the play is to be resumed after time, the chair umpire shall call "No time". (Sign)

• 11

The signs given by umpires and their postures during a match shall be as undermentioned.

(1) An umpire shall not give any signs in principle, when a ball is "in". In the case, however, where the ball was in, but in or out of the ball looks unclear to the players, the umpire in charge shall hold out its arm and hand forward with the palm facing downward as the sign of "in".

(2) The chair umpire shall not give any signs in principle. If required, however, the chair umpire may give signs in the same manner as those given by the vice umpire.

(3) The signs given by the viceumpire and its postures when judging a serve shall be as undermentioned.

a. The vice umpire's posture in judging a serve is forwarding a foot (at the receivers' side) and lowering its position and placing its hand (of the side where the foot forwarded) on the knee. To indicate the fault of a serve, excluding a netted serve which is out of its responsibility for judgment, the vice umpire shall raise its arm with fingers stretched out while keeping the posture.

In the case of a let in a serve, the vice umpire shall stand upright and raise one arm upward with two figures stretched, upward for a let in the first serve, and with one finger for the second serve, and make a call "Let".

b. When a ball in a rally has turned out to be out, the viceumpire shall take a position directly facing the landing spot of the ball and raise its one arm upright with all fingers stretched.

c. In the case of a point lost related to the other judgment items, the vice umpire shall point with one arm to the player of the point lost and make a call applicable to the judgment item.

d. When giving the sign of "no count" to the chair umpire, the vice umpire shall move its arms crossing in front of its face and make a call "No count".

e. Concerning "time", the vice umpire shall raise both of its arms upright with the palms facing toward the chair umpire, and make a call "Time".

(4) The signs given by the linesman shall be the same as those of the vice umpire.

(Verification of Judgment)

● 12

In the case where an umpire is not confident of the ball's "in" or "out" in its responsible judgment area, the umpire shall be allowed to make the judgment after checking the trace of the ball's landing on the ground. The chair umpire shall be allowed to request the vice umpire to check the trace, and if the vice umpire cannot be confident of its judgment, the chair umpire shall be allowed to come down from the umpire's chair and confirm the trace for itself to make the judgment.

(Coordination in Making Judgments)

● 13

In the case where an umpire cannot be confident of its judgment in its own judgment area, the umpire shall be allowed to ask for opinions from other umpires to verify its judgment.

(Final Judgment)

● 14

In the case where an inquiry about a judgment is made from a player during a match, the umpire in charge shall confirm the judgment and inform the result to the chair umpire, who shall declare the final judgment. After this process, any further inquiries about the final judgment shall be regarded as protests against the judgment, which shall be handled in accordance with the provisions of Articles 41 and 42 in the Rules for Competitions.

(Error in Judgment)

● 15

In the case where the judgment made by an umpire is recognized as an apparent error on the part of the umpire, the chair umpire shall be allowed to correct the judgment on that point.

(Suspension of Play)

● 16

In the case where an umpire has given a sign or a call to suspend a play erroneously while a ball in play, the chair umpire shall suspend the play at that instant. In the case where the erroneous sign or call was judged by the chair umpire to have caused a hindrance to the play, the point shall be a "no count", or a "let" if it was before the completion of a receive.

(Error in Score Counting)

● 17

In the case where any apparent error in point or game counting has been recognized, the umpire shall correct the count with a call "Correction" at the time when the first serve has turned fault or at the time of making a call on the next point. Even if the error has been found while a ball is in play, the play shall not be suspended and the point shall be effective.

(Default/Retirement)

● 18

In the cases where a player or pair has come under the provisions as undermentioned, the player or pair shall be treated as default on or retirement from the match and the victory of the opponent shall be declared. Points and games so far gained by such loser of the match as above shall be effective.

(1) An entry for competitions was made but the actual participation has not been made.

(2) A player or pair applied for default on or withdrawal from a match for some special reasons and the referee or the responsible competition official has accepted it.

(3) A player was allowed a time due to physical problems, but the player has failed to recover within the allowed time limits.

(4) A player applied for retirement from the ongoing match for physical problems and the chair umpire has accepted it.

(5) The competition has turned unable to be continued under the provisions of

Article 11 in the Rules for Operations of Competitions.

(Arousing of Attention)

● 19

The chair umpire shall be allowed to arouse the attention of people concerned (players, pairs, managers and teams) to their acts and others, if they are recognized as a hindrance to the smooth proceeding of a match.

(Warning)

● 20

In the case where the chair umpire recognized that a player, pair or manager in the case of an team event, has committed an apparent violation of Articles 15, 38 and 40 of the Rules for Competitions, the chair umpire shall issue a warning (yellow card) to such people as above. The warning shall be issued by showing the card.

(Disqualification)

● 21

(1) In the case where the referee found the violation of the conditions for participation described in the guide of competitions, the referee shall consult with the responsible competition official and, with a consent of the official, declare the disqualification of the player, pair or manager in the case of a team competition in question.

(2) In the cases as undermentioned, the chair umpire shall consult with the referee and, with a consent of the referee, disqualify the player, pair or team in the case of a team competition in question and then declare the victory of the opponent.

　　a. A player or pair who was called to appear on the court for a match, but has not appeared.

　　b. Players did not compete the matches in a team competition in accordance with the order which had been submitted in advance.

　　c. A player or pair has received warnings for 3 times during the same one match (Red Card).

(Prohibition of Replacement of Umpire)

● 22

The replacement of an umpire shall not be allowed, except the cases as undermentioned.

(1) The continuation of its duties has turned impossible due to physical problems.

(2) Participating players are umpiring and that situation is anticipated to make a hindrance to the proceeding of the competitions.

Chapter 4　Proceeding of Match

(Proceeding of Match)

● 23

The proceeding of a match shall be conducted in such manners as undermentioned under the guidance and directions of umpires.

(1) Both of the competing players or pairs shall stand behind and in the middle of the respective service lines, facing toward the net.

At this time, the chair umpire and the vice umpire shall stand outside the sideline on the side where the umpire's chair is placed, with the net between them. The linesmen to be in charge shall separately stand side by side and alongside the chair and vice umpires respectively.

(2) Following Item (1) above, the players shall proceed to the net by the chair umpire's signal. At the same time, the umpires shall also move toward the service center line along the net.

(3) At the net, the greetings shall be exchanged, firstly between the competing players and then with the umpires.

(4) After the greetings, the chair umpire shall identify each player for the match.

(5) In a team competition, all players of both competing teams shall line up behind the respective baselines, facing toward the net. By the chair umpire's signal, the two teams shall proceed to the net and exchange greetings. The managers of the teams, if applicable, shall stand nearest to the umpires. After the greetings by both of the two

teams, each of the matches in a tie shall be played one by one, just in the same manner as in the matches for individual events.

(6) After the greetings before the start of a match, the vice umpire, or the chair umpire if the vice umpire is dispensed with, shall show both of side A and B of a coin to each of the competing players and toss the coin up in the air. In the case where the side A of the coin came on the upper side when dropped on the ground, the player or pair at the right side of the chair umpire shall be given the preemptive right to choose service or receive side, and in the case where the side B of the coin came on the upper side, the player or pair at the left side of the chair umpire shall be given such preemptive right. The opposing player or pair to the owner of the preemptive right shall be given the right to choose among from the remaining options. For the convenience of an easier proceeding of competitions, the decision of serve/receive or side may be conducted in advance of a match at some other place than the court for the match.

(7) In the case where the choice of the kind of ball is applicable, the player or pair who has been given the preemptive right as provided in the preceding Article 23(6) shall be qualified for the ball selection. In the case of a team competition, the kind of ball which was decided by the representatives of both teams shall be used.

(8) After servers, receivers and sides were decided, the players shall exercise a warm-up practice before the start of the match. During this process, umpires shall take their respective, designated positions. The duration of the warm-up session shall usually be not longer than 1 minute. The referee shall be allowed, after consultation with the responsible competition officials, to reduce or omit the duration of the warm-up session, depending on the progress of competitions. Such decisions, once made, shall be informed to the umpires in charge.

(9) When the time allowed for a warm-up has elapsed, the chair umpire shall make a call "Ready" and urge the players to get ready for the start of the match.

(10) When the players are in a ready position for the start of the match, the chair umpire shall let the players start the match following calls like "Service side, Mr./Ms. -------of ----- (Club) and Mr./Ms. ------ of ----- (Club), Receive side, Mr./Ms. ------- of -----(Club) and Mr./Ms. -------- of ----- (Club), (Seven/nine) game match, play ball ".

(11) Umpires shall proceed with a match from the start and finish accurately and smoothly in accordance with the provisions of the Rules for Competitions and this Rules.

(12) When the match was completed, the chair umpire shall call "Game set". Then, the chair umpire shall get down from the umpire's chair and move along the net to the center of the court, together with other umpires, while calling the players to come to the net. Then, the chair umpire shall declare the result of the match by calling, for example, " This match to Mr./Ms. ------ and Mr./Ms. -------, with the score 7 to 4." Following this, the greetings shall be exchanged between the competing players and then with the umpires, and then they shall be dismissed.

(13) For a team competition, after all the matches in the tie are completed, all the players of both teams shall line up behind the baselines as they did before the start of the tie, and then proceed closer to the net. Then, the chair umpire shall declare the result of the tie by calling, for example, "This competition to -------- , with the score 2 to 1". Then, the greetings shall be exchanged between the two teams and then with the umpires, and then they shall be dismissed.

(Entering in Score Sheet)

● 24

The designated form of score sheet shall be used in principle for recording match results and filled in by the chair umpire during the match in accordance with the data entering manual. In the case, however, where sufficient time is not allowed to complete the score sheet after a "Game set" call and before the exchange of the final greetings with the players, the chair umpire shall make an effort to complete entering in the score sheet as soon as possible after the greetings.

Score Sheet Filling Guide

(1) The chair umpire shall fill in a score sheet accurately.

(Columns of Event, Court Number, Round, and Names of Players shall be entered in principle by the staff in charge in advance. The chair umpire shall confirm them and, in addition, shall enter the names of umpires in charge.)

(2) When the server (s)/receiver (s) are decided, the initials of S (for server) and R (for receiver) in the applicable columns shall be circled.

(3) In POINT columns, the mark "○" shall be entered for points won in the small squares and the mark " × " for points lost, starting from the upper left to rightward in the respective game columns.

(4) When a game is completed, the respective total points won for the game shall be entered in the central SCORE columns provided for each game, and the number of points won by the winner of the game shall be circled.

(5) When a match is completed, the respective total number of games won for the match shall be entered in the SCORE column which is provided between the columns for the names of competing players in the upper part of the form and the number of games won by the winner of the match shall be circled.

(6) In WARNING columns, the kinds of warning issued shall be entered by circling the initials of Y (for a yellow card) or R (for a red card) in the respective columns provided for competing players in the lower part of the form and remarks shall be filled in for reference to the warning issued . If applicable, warnings issued to a manger in the case of a team competition shall also be noted in these columns.

(7) In Time columns, the figure 5 (minutes) shall be circled for the respective players at each time "time" occurs for physical problems.

Rules for Operations of Competitions

Chapter 1　General Rules
(Purpose)

● 1

(1) This Rules shall be intended to provide the matters required for operations of soft tennis competitions (hereinafter "Competitions").

(2) A managing organization which is entrusted with operations of the Competitions by a host federation and a managing federation (hereinafter called the "host/managing organizations") shall conduct the operations based on this Rules in principle.

(Guide to Competitions)

● 2

The host/managing organizations shall prepare a guide to competitions and inform it to all the participants in advance. The contents of the guide to competitions shall be as follows in principle.

(1) Name of Competition

(2) Name of Host Organization

(3) Name of Managing Organization

(4) Name of Cooperative/Supporting Organizations

(5) Period of Competition

(6) Venue of Competition

(7) Place of Competition

(8) Items of Event

(9) Schedule of Competition

(10) Qualification of Participants

(11) Method of Entry (including Changes of Players after Entry)

(12) Rules for Competitions & Supplementary Regulations

(13) Method of Competitions and Determination of Ranking

(14) Preparation of Draw

(15) Conditions for Participation

(16) Balls and Other Equipment/Facilities

(17) Doping

(18) Medical Care

(19) Security

(20) Commendations

(21) Expenses for Participants

(22) Managers' Meeting

Chapter 2　Competition Facilities
(Competition Facilities)

● 3

The competition facilities shall be as follows in principle.

(1) The competition facilites shall include soft tennis courts and othe facilities (net, net posts and umpire's chair) and equipment (fences, benches, score boards, seats for spectaors, lavatories, players' waiting rooms, changing rooms, seats for competition officials, distinguished guests, reporters and medical care, court brushes, line brushes, flag

poles, showers and drinking water tanks, etc.).

(2) One court of the courts shall be designatd as the main court. The main court shall preferably be independent from the othe courts and have spectators' seats.

(3) The surface of court and out-court shall be clay, sanded artificial turf (grass) or all-weather chemical for outdoor courts, and wooden board, hard rubber or chemical for indoor courts. It shall be so written in the Guide to the Competitions.

(4) The courts shall be sufficient in number to complete all competitions depending on the scale of competitions or expected schedule.

(5) The place of benches in the courts shall be set in the outcourts to the extent that no hindrance to the play shall be caused.

Chapter 3   Competitons
(Items of Event)

● 4

The events of the competitions shall be decided by the host/managing organizations among from the events provided below and shall be written clearly in the guide to the competitions.

(1) Individual doubles for men and women

(2) Individual singles for men and women

(3) Individual mixed doubles

(4) Team competitions for men and women

(Schedule of Competitions)

● 5

The schedule of the competitions shall be decided by the host/managing organizations and shall be written clearly in the guide to the competitions.

(Qualifications for Participation)

● 6

The qualifications for participation shall be decided by the host/managing organizations and shall be written clearly in the guidlines to the competitions.

(Entry)

● 7

(1) The method of entry shall be decided by the host/managing organizations and shall be written clearly in the guide to the competitions.

(2) Change of player(s) after entry shall not be allowed in principle except for the case where its approval is given by the host/managing organizations. In this case, the host/managing organizations shall clarify this in the guide to the competitions.

(Special Cases Applicable to the Rules for Competitions)

● 8

The competitions shall be operated by the Rules for Competitions of Soft Tennis (hereinafter called the "Rules for Competitions") and the Rules for Umpiring of Soft Tennis (hereinafter called the "Rules for Umpiring") in principle, but the host/managing organizations may set up special cases as provided below. In this case, however, the host/managing organizations shall write clearly in the Guide to the competitions.

(1) Concerning the Rules for Competitions and the Rules for Umpiring, in the case where the domestic rules (so called "local rules") stipulated by the national association are available, such domestic rules may be applicable to the national competitions, etc.

(2) In the team competitions, one manager or coach shall be included in a team. In this case, the manager or the coach shall be regarded as one of the players of the team.

(3) In the team competitions, members of the team may enter into the permitted place in the court and may give advice or certain treatments for the physical accident under the conditions provided in the Rules for Competitions.

(Method of Competitions)

● 9

(1) The competitions shall be performed by one of the methods provided below, and it shall be decided by the host/managing organizations and be written clearly in the Guide to the competitions.

a. Tournament System (The final winner in the knockout system shall be the first place winner and the subsequent winners shall be determined in the same method.)

b. Round Robin System (All players or pairs shall compete each other and the ranking shall be decided by the method stipulated separately.)

c. Combination of both systems of the tournament and the round robin (Combination of the two systems of A and B above, depending on the scale of participation.)

(2) The method of team competitions shall be as provided below:

a. In either of tournament or round robin systems, the matches in the odd number shall be played in the order submitted in advance and the team which has won more wins than the opponent shall be the winner of the tie.

In this case, a tie shall consist of matches of singles or doubles or the combination of these two, and all the matches of the tie shall be played in principle. However, by the decision of the host/managing organizations, there may be the case where the team which has won more than one half of the matches in the tie shall be determined as the winner and the remaining match(es) shall not be played.

b. In case of causing shortage of team members in a team, if the team can play more than one half matches of the tie, the team can take part in the competition with approval by the referee and the responsible competition official. In this case, however, the matches shall be played starting with first match in accordance with the order submitted in advance, and the match(es) which can not played because of the player shortage shall be dealt with as default.

c. The number of games in a match shall be decided by the host/managing organizations and it shall be informed clearly to the participants in the guide to the competitions.

(Ranking in Round Robin Competitions)

- 10

The decision of ranking in the round robin shall be made by the methods as follows:

(1) Where two teams have the same win ratio, the winner of the competition between the two shall be ranked higher.

(2) Where three or more teams have the same win ratio, their rankings shall be determined by a comparison of the win ratios in the competitions between the three or more teams, and the team which has gained a higher win ratio shall be ranked higher.

(3) Where the method in (2) above cannot be implemented, rankings shall be

determined by a comparison within the competitions between the teams with the same win ratio, firstly of the number of games won minus the number of games lost, secondly of the number of points won minus the number of points lost and a player or a pair who has gained a larger positive differential shall be ranked higher. In the team competition, rankings shall be determined by a comparison, firstly of the number of matches won minus the number of matches lost, and secondly of the total number of games won minus the total number of games lost, and thirdly of the total number of points won minus the total number of points lost, and the team which has gained a larger positive differential shall be ranked higher.

In the case where such results of two teams are the same, Item 10 (1) above shall be applied.

(4) Where the method (3) above is not applicable, the host/managing organizations shall be allowed to determine the rankings by draw or other appropriate methods.

(How to Deal With Default in Round Robin Competition)

● 11

In the case where player (s) or pair (s) has (have) retired before the completion of the round robin in a team competition, the treatments shall be as undermentioned. In the case, however, where some other method decided by the host/managing organizations in advance is in place, the decision by this shall be applied firstly.

(1) In the case where more than one half of the players in a team have retired, the team shall not be able to continue the competition. In this case, all the results of the preceding matches shall be disregarded, resulting in the team's loss of the tie by a zero score retroactive to the first match of the tie. In the case, however, the retirement has been determined under Articles 39 of the Rules for Competitions and 18 of the Rules of Umpiring, the results so far made in the tie shall be kept effective.

(2) In the case where less than one half of the players in a team have retired in a tie, the team shall be allowed to continue the competition with an approval of the referee and the responsible competition official. In this case, the match(s) not played because of the retirement shall be regarded as lost by a zero score.

(3) In the case where a player or a pair is not able to continue the match for some reason before the completion of all matches in the round robin individual competition, the result of all the preceding matches shall be regarded as lost by a zero score. In the

case, however, where the retirement has been determined under Articles 39 of the Rules for Competitions and 18 of the Rules for Umpiring, the results so far made before the retirement shall be kept effective.

(4) In the case of coming back to the competition again after the retirement in the individual competition, the player or pair shall be allowed to continue the competition with an approval and directions of the referee and the responsible competition official. In this case, the result of match(es) not played shall be regarded as lost by a zero score.

(Retirement)

● 12

In the case applicable to Articles 39 of the Rules for Competitions and 18 of the Rules of Umpiring, the opponent shall be regarded as won the match. In this case the points and games so far won by the loser shall be kept effective.

(Disqualification)

● 13

(1) In the case applicable to Articles 42 of the Rules for Competitions and 21 of the Rules of Umpiring, the disqualification shall be applied retroactively to the first match of the competitions. The ranking gained by such a disqualified player shall be kept vacant.

(2) A team which comes under the preceding article in a team competition shall be disqualified.

(3) In a tournament system, a player, pair or team defeated by the disqualified player, pair or team shall not be able to come back.

(Draw)

● 14

The draw shall be decided fairly by the host/managing organizations in accordance with the following criteria in principle.

(1) Tournament System

a. In the case where the number of participants is the n'th power of 2 like 4, 8, 16, 32, 64, 128, 256, 512.

b. In the case where the number of participants is not the number of n'th power of

2 (base number), the base number which is the nearest larger number to the number of participants minus the number of participants shall be the number of byes, and the number of participants minus the numbers of byes shall be the number of the first round players. In a draw chart, the number of participants shall be divided into two, four or eight, and in the case of the odd number of participants, the odd number of participants shall be allocated to the block with a higher seed. In the case where one block consists of three participants, the player seeded higher in the block shall be allocated a bye.

(2) Round Robin System

a. Participants shall be divided into two or more blocks depending on the number of participants, if appropriate.

b. The seeding of all participants and a draw shall be decided in the same manner as in the tournament system and the applicable number of participants for each block shall be decided according to the draw. In the case where 16 participants, for example, are divided into four blocks, the seeding shall be arranged as follows:

Allocation By Block of the Seeded

1st Block	1	16	9	8
2nd Block	4	13	12	5
3rd Block	3	14	11	6
4th Block	2	15	10	7

c. Order of Matches in Round Robin System

* 3 Participants per Block 1-2, 2-3, 1-3

* 4 Participants per Block 1-2, 3-4, 1-3, 2-4, 2-3, 1-4

* 5 Participants per Block 1-2, 3-4, 2-5, 1-3, 4-5, 2-3, 1-4, 3-5, 2-4, 1-5

* 6 Participants per Block 1-2, 3-4, 5-6, 1-3, 2-5, 4-6, 3-5, 2-6, 1-4, 3-6, 2-4, 1-5, 2-3, 4-5, 1-6

The order of matches as above shall be finalized by the host/managing organizations of the competitions. In the case where the participants belonging to the same federation are allocated to the same block, a match between them shall be proceeded over the other matches regardless of the order of matches as above.

● 15

The host/managing organizations shall describe the record of match scores in the program in a manner as follows:

(1) Game scores shall be described for individual competitions.

(2) Match scores shall be described for team competitions.

(3) Regarding retirement, an initial "R" shall be noted on each column of the retired in the program, etc. together with their effective scores.

(4) Regarding disqualification, an initial "D" shall be noted in the programs, etc. on the applicable round column in the tournament and on all the applicable match columns in the round robin.

(5) In the case where any player, pair or team has changed since the completion of the program, the correction shall be made accordingly.

(Conditions for Participation)

● 16

All of the participants shall observe the conditions for participation decided by the host/managing organizations and specified in the guide to competitions.

(Balls for Competitions)

● 17

The host/managing organizations shall inform the kind of balls to be used in the competitions in the guide to competitions.

(Doping Test)

● 18

Implementation of the doping test at competitions, as applicable, shall be notified to the participants in the guide to competitions and the participants shall take the doping test in accordance with the provisions specified in the guide to competitions.

(Medical Care)

● 19

The host/managing organizations shall take into consideration to the extent possible a medical care for players and other people concerned, and shall prepare for providing the first aid treatment in case of emergency.

(Commendation)

● 20

The host/managing organizations shall inform the contents of commendation in the guide to competitions.

(Expenses for Participation)

● 21

In the case where the expenses for participation are to be charged to the participants, the detailed information on it shall be notified in the guide to competitions.

(Representatives' Meeting)

● 22

In the case where the representatives' meeting is to be held before the competitions in order to realize a smooth operation of the competitions, the host/managing organizations shall inform the time and date, purposes and required attendants etc. of the meeting in the guide to competitions.

(Competition Officials)

● 23

Competition officials shall be organized by the host/managing organizations in order to realize a smooth operation of the competitions, by refereeing to the 'Manual for Organizing Officials for Competition' which is provided separately.

(Jury)

● 24

(1)The Jury consists of referee(s) and umpires and shall be organized by the host/managing organizations.

(2) The referee(s) shall direct the umpires in conducting their fair judgment, and make an appropriate interpretation and application of the Rules for Competitions and the Rules for Umpiring.

(3)In the case where there are more than one referees, one of them shall be appointed as the chief referee.

(4)Umpires shall consist of one chair umpire and one vice umpire in principle and shall be organized with not less than 4 umpires in total for one court to be used for competitions in principle. The total number of umpires may be reduced, as appropriate, in the case where the host/managing organizations have decided not to place a vice umpire or to have participating players function for umpiring.

(5)Court supervisors shall be allowed to be placed, as required.

Chapter 4   Other Miscellaneous Matters
(Security)

● 25

The host/managing organizations shall try to keep smooth operations and security in the competitions by issuing ID-cards to players, officials and other people concerned in principle.

(Admission Fee)

● 26

The host/managing organizations shall be allowed to collect the admission fee for competitions.

(Sponsors)

● 27

The host/managing organizations shall be allowed to have sponsors. In this case, all the matters concerning sponsors shall be decided by the host/ managing organizations.

参考文献

[1] Asian Soft Tennis Federation. What is soft tennis [EB/OL]. [2021-1-5]. https://www.astf.asia/whatissofttennis.html.

[2] Asian Soft Tennis Federation. Organization [EB/OL]. [2021-1-5]. https://www.astf.asia/organization.html.

[3] Asian Soft Tennis Federation. Result [EB/OL]. [2021-1-5]. https://www.astf.asia/results.html.

[4] Korea Soft Tennis Association. Rule [EB/OL]. [2021-1-5]. http://softtennis.sports.or.kr/servlets/org/front/app20/action/app20_30.